DIVINING YOUR LIFE

Candle Readings with The Flame of Vesta

Debra May Macleod

© Debra May Macleod 2021

Book ISBN- 978-1-9994300-5-4
Ebook ISBN: 978-1-9994300-6-1

Cover design by Caroline Leger
Cover photo: Statue of Hestia(Vesta) © Romix Image, Shutterstock.com
Inside illustrations:
Stylized symbol of Vesta 4: design by Jeanine Henning
The Greek near a cup with fire © MariLila Shutterstock.com
Yellow melting candle © StefanFenech, Shutterstock.com
Life of sea watercolor painting © Melada photo Shutterstock.com
Ancient black and white compass © jittawait21 Shutterstock.com
From the author's collection:
Grids, photos and sample readings
Ancient Roman coin
Bronze of Vesta
PD   Illustration   Temple   of   Vesta:
https://commons.wikimedia.org/wiki/File:Trattato_generale_di_archeologia257.pn
g CC-PD. Temple of Vesta in Roman Forum, Illustrazione da Trattato di Archeologia, Iginio Gentile, Serafino Ricci, 1901.
PD Illustration of instrument from *Justi Lipsi de Vesta et Vestalibus Syntagma*

AllThingsVesta.com

TABLE OF CONTENTS

PREFACE

I sat curled up on the couch with my Greek friend, sipping Greek coffee, with a candle burning on the table in front of us.

"I think I'm done writing about ancient Rome and the Vestals for a while," I said. "Maybe I'll take a break."

"Yeah, right," she replied.

"No, I'm serious. Maybe I'll write about Tudor England. The six wives of King Henry or something…"

"I can't see it."

"Okay…the wives of the Inca."

"Warmer, but still no."

"What about—"

She sighed loudly enough to interrupt me and took the empty coffee cup out of my hand. She placed it upside down on the saucer. After a short time, she lifted the cup off the saucer and looked inside.

"What do you see?" she asked, gesturing to the sludge of coffee grinds that had run down along the sides of the cup, bottom to rim, to create a network of amorphous shapes and squiggly lines.

I studied the cup. My friend had read my coffee grinds many times—all the women in her family did—and I had often seen images in them, but this time I was struggling. "It looks like a Jackson Pollock painting," I said. "I don't see anything."

She let out an even more exasperated sigh, gathered our cups, and took them into the kitchen. "You'll get a sign," she said.

I sat back on the couch and stared absently at the candle on the coffee table. It was a beeswax tealight, sans casing, which I had set on a plate to burn.

As I looked at it, a small, thin, horizontal fracture appeared in the side of the wax, and a narrow river of amber wax spilled out. I blinked as the river quickly took the shape of the letter V. For *Vesta*.

I picked up the plate and turned it around, instantly noticing that, when I turned the plate 180°, the river of wax took on the shape of a...well, a *river*. Specifically, the Tiber River in Rome. And even more specifically, the shape of the bend in the Tiber where the basket of Rome's legendary founder Romulus came to rest.

And if that isn't a sign, I don't know what is.

Nor do I know what has brought you to this little book. Perhaps you're looking for a sign in your life, or perhaps you're looking for answers or meaning in a deeper sense.

Regardless, candle reading is an ancient and life-affirming practice that, although lesser known than reading tea leaves or reading the stars, is nonetheless a powerfully intuitive and beautiful way to discover, to *divine*, the answers you seek.

But more than just helping you answer certain questions, candle reading done with the flame of Vesta can bring a profound sense of peace, comfort and meaning to all areas of your life, from your relationships to your finances.

It can help you see through life's lies to find your own truth, and to face down those fears that might be holding you back in life.

In fact, I'd encourage you to start the process right now.

Go find a candle and light it. Now think about the questions that are on your mind or in your heart.

Think about the things you want to know or the reassurances you seek. Do they concern love? Money? A potential move? Perhaps you're pondering a major life choice of some kind or you're having to cope with a life change that has been thrust upon you.

Perhaps you need a favorable sign, something that can point you in the right direction for happiness. Or perhaps you need the opposite—an unfavorable sign, something that can help steer you away from making a mistake.

Think about that question or need for a while. And then start reading this book in earnest with your candle nearby.

Before you know it, you'll be getting a lot more than candlelight out of your candles. You'll be finding enlightenment there too—answers, understanding, inspiration, strength, and comfort.

Finally, I encourage you, as much as possible, to have fun as you engage in this illuminating form of divination. No, that may not always be possible—or the point—but candle reading should generally be undertaken in a spirit of openness and joy.

I wish you all the best as you begin!

They regard the fire as consecrated to Vesta because that goddess, being the earth and occupying the central place in the universe, kindles the celestial fires from herself.

- Dionysius Halicarnassus, Greek Historian, 60-7 BCE

CHAPTER ONE

Looking for Signs

Who is Vesta?

Vesta is the ancient Roman goddess of the home and hearth.

Symbolized and embodied by a sacred, eternal flame—the *aeterna flamma*—Vesta was, and still is, one of the heavyweights in terms of religious importance. And before you use her sacred flame in divination, I believe it's essential to know a little bit about her, her history, and how she is honored today. Because it's pretty amazing.

Vesta is one of the *Dii Consentes*, the twelve ancient deities—six gods and six goddesses—of the ancient Roman pantheon (the others are Jupiter, Mars, Mercury, Neptune, Vulcan, Apollo, Juno, Minerva, Ceres, Diana, and Venus). This more or less aligns with the Greek pantheon of the twelve Olympic gods.

According to legend—and there is always far more truth in that than we think—during the fall of Troy, the hero Aeneas was able to save his doomed city's most important religious items, including sacred embers of Vesta's fire which burned in the Trojan hearth. Eventually his descendant, Romulus, brought the sacred flame to his new city, the city that took his name—Rome. There, a circular temple was built to house Vesta's eternal fire, its shape a reflection of the round huts the ancient Romans first called home, as well as the Earth itself, that place we all call home: it encircled the sacred fire as our planet circles the sun. This temple was one of the first to be erected in the Roman Forum (sometime in the 8th century BCE), and the Eternal City thus grew up and around the fiery goddess's Eternal Flame.

Because Vesta's sacred hearth was the hearth of Rome itself, Romulus's successor, King Numa, decreed that a powerful priesthood of Vestal Virgins keep the fire burning, day and night. Their devotion, and the rites and rituals they performed, maintained the *pax deorum*—the peace between humankind and the gods—as well as the protection of the gods. The Vestal Order was the only full-time, state-funded priesthood in Rome, and its priestesses enjoyed a life of privilege during their thirty years of service. After completing their service, they were free to retire as wealthy, independent women and even marry (they would be between thirty-six and forty years old at retirement), although many chose to remain with the order.

As the Kingdom of Rome expanded to become the Roman Republic and finally the great Roman Empire, so too did the sacred fire expand, with Vesta continuing to find new lands, and new hearths, in which to reside.

Yet Vesta was not just honored in the public sphere or at the state level. She was also—and originally—honored privately in each and every home, her presence in the family hearthfire and/or candles making even the most modest home a sacred space. Offerings of bread or salted flour, or libations of olive oil, wine, or milk, were given to her flame at mealtime and during times of prayer. Her flame symbolized eternity, home, and the soul.

Now as you might expect from a goddess symbolized by an eternal flame, Vesta was and is an enduring force. As such, she is still honored today, as are many other ancient gods and goddesses in the so-called neo-pagan movement. She is also honored by many people who don't identify as neo-pagan or pagan, but who simply feel drawn to her flame, and who use it as a spiritual focus. This too is to be expected in a world where more and more people identify as "spiritual, but not religious."

Fire worship is the oldest form of spiritual expression known to humankind: adding a little sophistication to this worship, and a face to the flame, brings comfort and meaning to many people. The complex rituals and rites that once attended Vesta have been adapted and simplified to suit modern lifestyles and sensibilities, and the fact that Vesta is honored privately rather than publicly.

For example, symbolic offerings and libations can be made to a Vesta-dedicated candle—that's something I'll expand on later in the book should you wish to incorporate it into your own life and spiritual practice, including candle reading.

In *Divining Your Life*, we're going to focus on burning Vesta's sacred *flamma* in a candle and then "reading" both the flame and the resultant candle wax drippings to discover—to divine—the answer to any number of life's questions. As you'll see, the method I use to do this, the method you'll learn to use, is one that stems from actual ancient practices and the deepest reaches of antiquity.

Modern Divination

Life is a mystery. And like any mystery, people are always trying to solve it, to reveal its secrets, to find answers to its many questions. Divination provides a way to do that.

Divination is commonly and very generally understood as the practice of trying to foresee future events, to answer certain questions, or to discover some kind of hidden knowledge by the interpretation or reading of signs, particularly signs from deities or other supernatural forces. It is the practice of revealing the hidden significance of events or choices in our own life.

Yet the heading I've used here—modern divination—is something of a misnomer. That's because most forms of divination practiced today originated in ancient times. That's very true of practices such as astrology and as you'll soon see, candle readings.

Perhaps one of the "newest" forms of popular fortune-telling or divination today is Tarot cards, which began to be used for divination purposes in the late 18th century CE—not ancient, but old.

But that's not to say the modern world hasn't come up with novel ways to divine answers to life's questions, big and small. Who can resist asking Mattel's Magic 8-Ball a question and frantically shaking it, peering into that little round window to see the triangle-shaped answer—*Signs point to yes.*

What schoolboy hasn't quietly created a paper fortune-teller, commonly called a cootie catcher, at his desk during algebra class? What schoolgirl hasn't consulted the Daisy Oracle—*he loves me, he loves me not*—to let the petals say whether her crush is reciprocated?

And aren't many of us tempted to ask a question of the Ouija board, despite the dark tones some associate with it? Like Tarot, however, spirit boards weren't popularized as a method of divination until relatively recently: they were originally a parlor game and began to be used for séance purposes in the late 19th century CE.

We are likewise drawn to those who appear to have mastered divination. Nostradamus, who lived in the 16th century CE, is believed to have accurately prophesized a number of major world events, including the French Revolution and the rise of Adolf Hitler.

In a lighter vein, Paul the Octopus predicted the results of a number of football matches in the early 2000's and gained a tongue-in-cheek reputation as an animal oracle, attracting crowds of onlookers who eagerly awaited his startlingly accurate predictions.

Yet the truth is, from the crystal ball to runes, from tea-leaf readings to numerology, from Tarot to talking boards, and from the predictions of serious French seers to silly psychic cephalopods, almost all modern divination methods took root in the ancient world in one way or another.

After all, those people who lived before us, even millennia before us, wanted to solve the same mysteries that we do. Some of those mysteries are serious—what is the meaning of my life?—while others are trivial—which team should I bet on?—but either way, we instinctively turn to divination to discover the answers.

Even those methods of divination that may seem flippant—like the Magic 8-Ball—are thus deeply instinctual and stem from ancient yearnings and practices.

In modern times, these practices may have grown and adapted, they may have found their way onto store shelves and the Internet, and at times even infiltrated pop culture. Nonetheless, they're old. Really old.

And the divination practice of candle reading—specifically the type based in ancient Roman religion and using the flame of Vesta—is one of the *very* oldest. It's one of the *most* ancient. And in my opinion, it's the most beautiful.

By divining a classical element—fire, and its effects—you're reaching far back into the human experience, into distant antiquity. In fact, you're reaching even further back than that, all the way back to the dawn of human spirituality itself.

The Spirituality of Fire

Fire worship is one of the oldest, if not *the* oldest, forms of spiritual expression known to humankind. It is around fire that the earliest humans built their social and family units, built their homes, built their cultures and civilizations.

They built their religions around fire too. Who among us does not feel a sense of that ancient spiritual reverence when she looks into a moving orange flame in the dark?

Who does not experience a sense of awe when he feels the heat radiate into his body, hears the crackle of the fire, or watches a burning ember snap out of the flames to fly upward into the heavens to join the stars, those fires in the sky?

What began as dances and chants around the fire—early rituals to celebrate and appease the fire gods—eventually grew into the sophisticated religion of Vesta with her complex rites and rituals, and her esteemed order of professional priestesses.

What began as a circle of stones around a fire on the ground just outside a rocky cave eventually grew into the circle of white marble that comprised the Temple of Vesta and housed the sacred fire, an eternal fire that burned within a round bronze firebowl.

From our distant ancestor hominids in the Stone Age to the innovative people of the great Roman Empire, to the person reading this book in the modern Digital Age of the 21st century CE, there is a common spiritual thread—a reverence for fire binds us together.

Ancient Divination

The ancient world and the modern world are separated by years, but not by yearning. Like us, the ancients wanted to discover the mystery of life and to know the unknown. To do that, they, like us, often turned to divination. They, like us, looked for "signs."

The ancient Romans, in particular, had a penchant for looking for and reading signs to divine the will of the gods. They looked for signs everywhere and in nearly everything, and they lived by them in both their private and public lives.

They drew lots (*sortes*) at Praeneste and rolled the dice in taverns. Those who had the means consulted great oracles, such as at Delphi, while others relied on street-corner soothsayers. They read the entrails of sacrificed animals (this practice was called *haruspicy*). They interpreted prodigies and omens such as spontaneous lightning strikes, strange animals, and eclipses, and they consulted astrologers.

If the signs were favorable, they would marry so-and-so—if not, they would refuse. If the signs were favorable, they would go to war—if not, they would refrain. They studied the signs and saw patterns in them, and since they continued to do this for centuries, it must have proven itself useful!

While ancient writers like Livy, Plutarch, Gellius and others give us glimpses into ancient Roman divination, it is the Roman statesman Marcus Tullius Cicero who gives us one of the most complete sources of information in his book called *De Divinatione* or "on divination."

Written in the 1st century BCE, it is a varied and illuminating read, one set up as something of a philosophical debate. In it, Cicero relates that all people, both refined and rough, from the Assyrians to the Egyptians, have practiced divination. That is, even those who were ancient to those we consider ancient practiced divination!

Ancient Augury

In *De Divinatione*, Cicero points out that Romulus himself was very skilled at a certain type of divination known as *augury*. Augury was of central importance to Roman religion and the state itself. In its simplest terms, it was the practice of interpreting the will of the gods by looking for *auspicia*, or signs, in the sky—things like lightning or the flight of birds. This was called "taking the auspices" and it is where we get our word auspicious. It is a practice the Romans may have borrowed and adapted from the Etruscans, although various cultures practiced it.

Although a complex ritual with a plethora of rigid rules (and at times confusing or conflicting accounts of those rules), I'll run through a very general introduction to the practice.

Taking the auspices involved a skilled type of priest, called an *augur*, using a special curved staff, called a *lituus*, to mark out a section of the sky. This section of the sky was called a *templum,* and it was within this sacred space that the augur would carefully and skillfully watch for signs from the gods.

It is from the term templum, and this concept, that we get the words *temple* and *contemplation*, both of which communicate the presence of the divine and the need for reverent, thoughtful behavior.

Facing south (or east—the orientation is a complex matter, and I'll expand upon this important point as we move along), the augur would divide the sky into sections or quarters, with the left-hand side of the augur being to the east and the right-hand side to the west. The area behind the augur was of course to the north.

To aid the augur in the intense concentration necessary to read the signs, it was necessary that a distraction-free state of silence be achieved. Finally, the augur would wait and watch for signs.

There were two types of signs that might be seen. One was *auspicia impetrativa*: these were sent by the gods in response to questions deliberately and diligently asked of them. The other type was *auspicia oblativa*: these were spontaneous, unsolicited signs sent by a deity to approve or disapprove of something.

Generally, it was held that signs which appeared to the left of the augur—perhaps a roll of thunder or a flock of a certain type of bird—were favorable signs. Signs on the right were unfavorable.

Again, this is only a superficial description of augury. It was a complicated, formal practice that was used in various capacities and for different purposes—from whether to launch a military campaign to whether to marry a certain someone—and it had an exhaustive catalogue of terminology, procedures and rules (and exceptions) when it came to observing and interpreting the signs.

My purpose here is simply to introduce you to the basic concept of the practice because we will be using it to some extent, and because this form of divination was so important to the ancients who honored Vesta's sacred flame.

In fact, Romulus, who was the son of a legendary Vestal priestess named Rhea Silvia, used a form of auspices called *ex avibus*—divination through the flight of birds—to determine where to found his city. The appearance of twelve vultures in the sky over the Palatine Hill assured him that the gods were marking the spot from above.

The observation and interpretation of the flight of birds was very common, and like all forms of augury, had its peculiarities: a raven on the normally unlucky right was actually a good sign, while a crow on the normally lucky left was a bad sign.

Another form of auspices that I previously touched on is what the ancient augurs called *ex caelo*—signs from the heavens or the sky, and specifically signs from Jupiter, god of the sky.

Once the augur marked out the templum in the sky and asked his question, he would watch and wait. A flash of lightning on a clear blue day, especially one on the left, might be taken as an encouraging "yes" from the father of the gods, while an ominously shaped cloud that suddenly formed on the right might be taken as a warning—"don't do it."

Ex Flamma: Signs & the Sacred Fire

As an author of historical fiction who writes about ancient Rome and the Vestal Virgins, I've tried to immerse myself in their world. I've done endless hours of research, studied statues, relief carvings and archeological discoveries. I've delved into numismatics so that I can hold and study the coins the ancients held. I've visited Rome many times to walk in the footsteps of the Vestals, through the Forum and the House of the Vestals, and spent hours at the ruins of the temple. I've been lucky enough to receive special access into (and under) some incredible spaces during the course of my authorship, including being able to step "inside" the ruins of Vesta's temple to stand in the very spot where the sacred fire once burned.

That was an emotional experience for me. It was amazing to look around and imagine being enclosed by the circular marble walls, with the eternal fire burning in its hearth and its smoke slipping out the oculus in the domed roof. I could picture the Vestal Virgins standing over the fire, murmuring their prayers to the goddess and making offerings into the flames.

Some valuable knowledge about ancient Roman religious practices has come down to us from various sources, including those practices that involved the Vestals. For example, we know some of the festivals and rites they participated in, we know about the sacred cakes they made, we know what it took to be a Vestal, and we know about their privileges and punishments.

We know the sacred fire was ceremoniously extinguished and renewed every March 1st, the first day of the New Year, according to the old Roman calendar. The ancient historian Plutarch, when writing about the sacred fires at Delphi and Rome, suggests the new fire was drawn from sunbeams. This was done using a polished brass instrument that caught the rays of the sun and ignited the tinder. Others say the fire was renewed using wood friction, specifically the branches from an oak tree that was sacred to Jupiter.

Yet as much as we do know, there is much more that we don't know. Many of the rites and rituals the Vestal priestesses performed over the sacred fire were done in secret, within the walls of Vesta's temple, and as such we know precious little about those.

Because of the secrecy involved in the Vestals' duties and the lack of detailed knowledge about inner temple practices, I had to fill in a lot of gaps in my novels if I wanted to flesh out living characters and bring "temple life" to life. This much I knew: the Romans were an extremely pious and diligent people. To maintain the pax deorum, they had a vast array of formal prayers, petitions, rites, rituals, habits, customs, and protocols. It is therefore inconceivable that the Vestals would have been content with simply piling wood on the fire, saying a prayer or two, and leaving it at that.

Rather, they would have had an inventory of religious rituals and prayers that they performed daily over the sacred fire to secure the protection of Vesta. They would have had special rites and rituals to use in times of crisis, whether war or plague or invasion.

To immerse myself in a Vestal's world, I therefore used what I knew about Roman religion and Vesta to create not only prayers, rites and rituals gleaned from various authentic sources, but also to create a plausible method of fire divination wherein the priestesses read signs in the sacred fire as it burned in its circular firebowl.

I reasoned that, since the augurs looked for signs that came from Jupiter and his abode in the heavens (*ex caelo*), the Vestals would surely have looked for signs that came from Vesta and her home in the fire, and so I called this latter form of auspices *ex flamma*. Signs *from* or *out of the flame*.

There is no doubt that the Vestals would have sought Vesta's presence and guidance in the flames, gauging whether the goddess was pleased or not, or whether more needed to be done to secure her protection. They would have sought out her wisdom and judgment, and striven to appease her on behalf of Rome and its ruler, army and people.

They would have carefully watched and listened for a notable flare, sway or whoosh of a flame, or a crack of an ember, and they would have diligently recorded and interpreted those signs, thus divining the will of the goddess via *pyromancy*. Pyromancy is a word that comes to us from the Greek *pyr* (fire) and *manteia* (divination): so quite literally, it means divining through fire. The Vestals would also have looked for signs in the smoke, noting its density, shape and how it moved. They would have collected the burnt wood and ash and looked for signs in those too.

To add detail and formality to this fire-based method of divination, I adapted certain other elements of augury, including the idea of creating a templum in which to observe and record the signs.

I imagined that the firebowl in the temple was an earthly reflection of the heavens above—after all, the stars are, in their own way, fires in the sky. This meant that a Vestal could read the signs in the sacred fire in the same general way that an augur read the signs in the sky. The Vestal might look for spontaneous signs in the fire (*auspicia oblativa*) or ask the goddess a deliberate, specific question and observe the flames for an answer (*auspicia impetrativa*).

Standing behind the altar and facing east—the most likely direction, as the morning sunlight could have streamed directly onto the sacred fire through the open doors, thereby uniting cosmic and earthly fire—the Vestals could note in which directions and sections of the bowl the flames burned stronger or snapped louder.

A loud snap—the voice of Vesta—emanating on the left and thus from the north would be a fortunate or lucky sign: that's because the north was the direction in which the gods were said to reside in the sky. On the other hand, a strange sizzle heard on the right and thus to the south might be interpreted as unfavorable, or even as a sign of impending doom, one that might have the chief Vestal quickly consulting with the Pontifex Maximus. The same criteria would apply if more blackened wood or ash appeared in this or that section of the firebowl, or whether this or that section of the bowl became scorched.

When a Vestal's watch in the temple was over, she would convey any strange or unusual signs to the Vestal who was taking her place. In this way, they would always know whether Rome had the favor of the goddess or whether the pax deorum was threatened.

It is likely the Vestals would also have read the signs for important individuals, as well as for the state. From the emperor and empress to senators and wealthy merchants, people would have petitioned the Vestals to ask the goddess a private question on their behalf, and to read the flames and burnt wood to determine the will of the goddess. No doubt this was done in exchange for a healthy "donation." The Vestals were wealthy women, remember!

While this is just a quick overview of the divination system I researched and developed for my book series, it's enough to give you a general sense of my philosophy and approach. Soon, you'll soon see how all of this is relevant to *you* in terms of candle reading as you learn how to adapt and apply this methodology to read the flame, wax drippings, and vapor of candles.

Candle reading is a unique form of divination which can be performed in a variety of ways, and which requires a blend of art and skill. I've systemized all of that in this book, and I've done so in a way that incorporates actual ancient customs and the sacred flame of Vesta. Of course, the types of questions that you'll be divining will be very different. I don't anticipate you'll be asking questions like "Should Caesar expand the empire?" or "Will Senator Vibius's gout abate anytime soon?"

Your questions will undoubtedly be very personal and emotional. In fact, that's why I wrote the next chapter, chapter two, and encourage you to read it, to think about it, before you move on to subsequent chapters that will immerse you in the methodology, procedure, and interpretive aspects of detailed candle divination.

The flame of Vesta is a powerful force, but you can make your divination even more powerful and purposeful by doing a little soul-searching groundwork first.

Candle Reading: The Old Ways & the New

Before we move on, I'd like to talk about a few established methods of candle reading, since these do factor into the method I've created. *Carromancy* is a form of divination that looks for signs by reading the wax drippings of a candle while or after it burns. The word comes to us from the Greek *carro* (waxen, or molten) and *manteia* (divination).

Carromancy can also be performed by dropping wax drippings into a bowl of water and reading the shapes, movement, etc. of the droplets. When this latter approach is taken, elements of *hydromancy* (the term for divination using water) are also incorporated; however, it is not hydromancy in a true or exclusive sense, since the focus is not really on the water. Rather, the water is used as a suspending medium. The spotlight is on the wax drippings.

Another related practice that may or may not be incorporated into the carromancy divination ritual is *capnomancy* (from the Greek *capnos* or smoke). This is a form of divination that uses smoke or smoke vapor.

Carromancy is a very old practice, one that may have originated with the ancient Romans as they were probably the first to have put wicks in candles. Early Romans dipped wicks made of papyrus (a type of thick paper derived from plants) in beeswax, using the resultant candles to illuminate their homes and to perform religious rituals with. The word candle comes to us from the Latin *candela* or *candere*, which means "to glow."

While it is a lesser known method of divination than astrology or even Tarot card readings, carromancy is nonetheless still widely practiced by many cultures, religions and faiths. Some even see it as a form of magic. There is something instinctual that draws all people to a flame, including to the flame of a candle. There is indeed something magical about it!

Because candle reading is so widely and diversely practiced, many different methods, parameters and interpretations may be found. These will depend on the faith or discipline of the practitioner or the person performing the reading.

In this book, you'll learn about my particular candle reading methodology, parameters and approach, one that relies upon the sacred flame of Vesta.

As you will see, it incorporates the four candle-reading divination practices I've just mentioned: pyromancy, carromancy, hydromancy, and capnomancy. It also incorporates the fundamental elements of ancient Roman augury, which I've already outlined and which you'll learn to utilize in later chapters. You'll also see that it relies heavily on other aspects of ancient Roman symbolism while taking full advantage of what contemporary candles have to offer.

In this way, I have merged the past and the present to create a beautiful, meaningful and extremely enjoyable system of candle-reading divination, one that reflects and respects the goddess of fire, Vesta. To me, this is a wonderful way to blend the traditions of the ancient world with the possibilities and sensibilities of the modern world. **Because a candle is the new altar fire.**

CHAPTER TWO

Asking the Right Questions

The Purpose:
What Do You Want to Know?

Candles are used in countless capacities across religions and spiritual systems, from Catholicism and Neopaganism to Buddhism and Wicca, and many others. They may be used to remember the soul of a loved one or to commune with a deity, depending on your beliefs and your purpose.

In this book, the purpose is to use candles that burn with Vesta's flame for divination: to help you discover certain things about your life, and to answer questions that you have about it.

Candle divination can be a lighthearted and fun ritual. I love to sit around with friends, a glass of wine or cup of coffee in hand, and perform a divination for each of them. It might be a fairly long reading with a pillar candle, or it might be something quicker, like reading wax drippings in water. Either way, it gives us something interesting to focus on while we enjoy each other's company…and the questions each person asks can be quite revealing!

Yet candle divination—especially the method I detail in this book—has a more serious, spiritual purpose to it as well. It is a formal yet personal ritual, one that can help you gain insight into your life, tap into your intuition, and thus reveal what decisions are right or wrong for you, or which path you should or shouldn't take.

Its purpose is to discover and divine various aspects and areas of your life—past, present, and future—so that you can live a divine life. A peaceful, prosperous, and full life.

Its purpose is to ask the spirit of one of the most powerful goddesses of the ancient world, Vesta, to do what she does best—to speak to you from her eternal flame, and to guide and protect you.

Just as her flame once burned in the Temple of Vesta in the Roman Forum, just as it once burned in the hearth fires and candles of women and men in the ancient world, it now burns in *your* candle. It is that power and purpose that you can use in your own life.

Yet before you ask Vesta a question and use that power, it is wise to do a little soul-searching and ask yourself some questions first. What do you *really* want to know? Why? The Vestals and other ancient priests put great thought into the questions they asked the gods. They knew the true purpose of the questions they asked and they chose their words carefully. You should do the same.

You know what it means to shed light on a matter. It means to see something clearly. To have the truth revealed. If you ask the right questions of Vesta's flame, you will find the divination ritual can shed light on many matters and reveal many truths.

Love & Relationships

It's inevitable. If I have a group of friends over, at least one of them is going to say, "Do a candle reading for me! Ask if it's going to work out with this guy I'm seeing" or "Ask if he really loves me."

If it isn't a question about dating, it's a question about married life. "Should we move abroad?" Usually it's a hopeful or fun question. Sometimes it's less so. Sometimes it's downright dreary: "Is my partner cheating on me?" Or "Should I ask for a divorce?"

I've fielded a lot of relationship questions in my day. As a marital mediator by trade, I'm no stranger to the agonies and ecstasies that attend romantic relationships.

If you have a relationship question, Vesta's flame can be a guiding light for you. Just be clear about the question you're asking.

For example, the question "Will I meet someone new by spring?" is quite vague…you know what you mean, but it's still a really amorphous question. After all, the "someone new" you meet might be the biggest narcissist this side of the Atlantic and the worst dating disaster of your life.

A better question might be "Will I meet a quality romantic partner by June of this year?" Be clear about what you really want and why you want it. Give the signs good information to work with.

After you invoke Vesta and ask your question (don't worry, you'll learn how to do this soon), and while you await the signs, you should use the time to reflect, by the light of the flame, on your past or present relationship(s) or partner(s), as well as yourself.

While you're in this state of peaceful clarity, the flame and your intuition can work together to divine the answer. Every drip of wax, every sputter of the flame, will bring you closer to the truth.

During the silence of the ritual, as the flame melts the wax to leave signs behind, reflect upon your relationship issues.

If you are in a relationship and having struggles, ask yourself whether you are being the best version of yourself that you can be. Have you been asking too much of your partner or have you been letting them away with too much? Why?

If you're single and seeking—or at least keeping one eye open—ask yourself whether you tend to choose or pursue partners who are a good fit for you. Do you lack self-confidence or self-love?

These are general questions that may have a lot, a little, or nothing at all to do with your particular situation. That's okay. My point is to encourage you to make your divination ritual an active, not strictly passive, experience. The flame must be able to explore your thoughts and feelings, so make a connection with it.

A candle divination ritual can also help you gain insight into the various non-romantic relationships in your life, such as the relationships you have with family, friends, or colleagues.

It can help you ponder any estrangements with family or friends. You might ask, "Should I reconnect with my mother?"

This question in particular shows why it's so important to know the purpose of your question. Are you asking because you are being "guilted" or pressured into reconnecting? Or are you asking because you miss this person and believe it's a healthy decision?

But what if you don't have a specific question in mind? That's all right—you'll learn how to do general readings as well, during which you'll find answers to questions you didn't even know you should be asking.

Finances & Success

Love and money. Most of us spend a good portion of our adult lives thinking about them. I suppose that's why questions about finances are second only to questions about love when it comes to divination. Yet as with matters surrounding love and relationships, questions about money also need to be very clearly stated and may require some self-reflection.

For example, if you're tempted to ask Vesta the question "Am I going to be rich?" she may take this to mean "Will I own a private island staffed entirely with underwear models?" while you simply meant "Will I have enough money to own a home and take a tropical vacation every year?"

Rich is a subjective thing. The gods may have a much higher threshold than you do! As a result, you may get a false-negative reading—no, you won't be rich enough to own a private island ….but you will have the financial security to own a beautiful home and take wonderful vacations every year. That's rich enough for many people!

So know your question! And know yourself too.

Know thyself. It's a Delphic maxim, one that commands humankind to practice self-reflection and self-awareness. What in the world are Delphic maxims, you ask? Well, they are a set of ancient moral principles that were inscribed on the Temple of Apollo at Delphi and ascribed to the Oracle.

And this maxim's association with divinity and the Oracle shows how intimately self-reflection and intuition are connected with divination.

After you invoke Vesta and ask your question of her, and as the flame melts the wax to leave signs behind, you should therefore continue to ask yourself questions that will help the flame and your intuition divine the answer.

"What are my spending habits? What changes must I make in my life to have more money?" You get the idea. Who knows? Maybe the flame and the signs will spark a creative and profitable idea in your mind, or a brilliant entrepreneurial plan, something that will inspire you to get to work and add some zeros to the number on your bank statement!

Or perhaps the flame and the signs will ask you to look inward and to examine not just your spending habits, but your emotional relationship with spending.

I fully admit that I've made emotional purchases—what better way to soothe a disappointment than to purchase an expensive designer handbag? That might be okay once in a while, but few of us can afford to make a habit of it.

So whether you ask a specific question about money or you're doing a general reading and money is on your mind, don't just look for signs that say "jackpot" or "poverty," but rather look for signs that reflect your financial past, present, and future. Look for signs that have a personal, meaningful message to convey.

Because when it really comes down to it, success is a subjective thing to measure, isn't it?

On one hand, when we talk about someone who has a lot of money in the bank we say they "have a fortune."

On the other hand, when we talk about someone who has a lot of happiness in their life—friends, family, health, purpose, and so on—we say they "are fortunate."

The ancient Roman goddess of luck is named Fortuna. You may know her by her nickname, Lady Luck. In antiquity, people prayed to her not just for financial luck (Mercury was the go-to god for that), but they especially prayed to Fortuna for the kind of good fortune that we instinctively know leads to a successful life.

True success in life comes from being happy. From having meaningful relationships—not just a romantic relationship, but meaningful relationships with friends, family, our kids, colleagues, even our pets.

So as you seek to divine the signs that can help you have greater success in life, do some thinking and get clear about what success really means to you.

Career & Purpose

Career-focused questions are also commonly asked during divination. That makes sense. Our career is a big part of our life, and even our identity.

Think about it: when you meet someone new, the first question they ask you is "What's your name?" The second question they ask you is "What do you do for a living?"

When I graduated from law school, I thought, "Ah, now I get to have an important career. I'll impress others and be happy at the same time!" But guess what? Neither of those things happened.

First of all, trying to impress others is about the most pointless, time-wasting, soul-sucking, self-sabotaging pursuit you could possibly undertake in this life. No one cared that I had a law degree. They were too busy caring about their own lives.

And when I decided to abandon a law career in favor of a more autonomous career in mediation, and then ultimately a career in writing, no one—other than those closest to me—cared about that either.

Living to impress others is an empty pursuit. I thank the gods every day that I realized that, and I hope you've come to the same liberating realization in your life.

It doesn't matter whether you place a name plate with a fancy job title on your desk or whether you post a thousand fake-happy-perfect-life photos to social media—nobody is impressed. Not really. Not in any way that matters. Not for very long.

Moreover, during my time at law school and working in a law firm, I saw absolutely no evidence that an "impressive" career or job title would lead to happiness. Not a single shred of evidence.

Lawyers and other impressive career types aren't any happier than anyone else. In fact, some of the most impressive careers out there come with the least impressive happiness ratings. From divorce to depression, there is no guarantee that an impressive job title will make you happy on a personal level.

Now, if you are in fact a professional with an impressive job title and you're living the fulfilling life and career of your dreams, great! I am happy for you. I am also willing to bet that you truly love what you do. You find excitement or meaning in it. Even if the pay and prestige are great, you also find purpose in it.

And that's the point I'm leading up to. The happiest worker bees are those who find purpose in what they're doing. And it doesn't have to be some kind of lofty or humanitarian purpose either. If you feel that your career or your job gives YOU a purpose and serves a purpose in YOUR LIFE then, well, you are fortunate.

So by all means, ask career-focused questions during your candle divination ritual. Just make sure you're clear about what will make you truly happy in life. Once you're clear about that, look for signs that will point you down a career path with purpose.

Health & Well-Being

Good health is definitely a blessing in life. And while some health issues are beyond our control, there are lifestyle habits that can influence everything from our weight to our longevity. The silent focus that you'll experience during a candle divination ritual can be an incredibly helpful way to tune-in to your own body, to reflect upon your lifestyle habits, and to think about whether you're treating your physical body as well as you should.

But as we all know, being healthy isn't just a state of body. It's also a state of mind. It's an emotional and spiritual state. Yet too often, we don't reflect upon our mental, emotional, or spiritual well-being in the same way.

I mention this because I've done candle readings where a person has said "Ask whether I'll live a long life…I want to know!" Well, don't we all?! Then again…do we?

All of this calls to mind the ancient story of Prometheus. Prometheus was a Titan, the deity of forethought, who gifted mankind with the knowledge of how to use fire.

The Greek god Zeus, characteristically cheerless about the whole thing, punished Prometheus for this by chaining him to a cliff where each day an eagle would eat out his liver and each night it would grow back so that poor Prometheus could suffer the same torment the next day (but don't worry, he was eventually rescued by the hero Hercules during one of his twelve labors).

Because punishing Prometheus wasn't quite enough to let Zeus lay the whole matter to rest, he also punished mankind. To do this, he gave a jar to a woman named Pandora, telling her to not open it. But hey, you know women…we have to know…so of course she opened it, and when she did, out flew all the miseries of the world— including humankind's knowledge of its own mortality. To this day, we are burdened with the knowledge of it.

Yet as luck would have it, Pandora was able to close the jar, trapping one important thing inside—hope. That is why no matter how bad things get in life we always have hope.

Focusing on hope, being a hopeful person, is certainly more productive and inspiring than trying to prophesize one's life expectancy! Talk about depressing.

So hope for the best. Take care of yourself and use the divination ritual to look for signs that can help you take even better care of yourself.

That includes taking care of your mental, emotional and spiritual health, as well as your physical health. Instead of asking "Will I live a long life?" think about asking "Am I as healthy as I can be right now in all areas of my life?"

And by the way, don't forget to get a good night's sleep! Sleep is an incredibly important part of health and well-being. A good night's sleep can help heal the body, while our dreams, good or bad, can help us process the day's events and emotions.

Dreams can be so useful and powerful, in fact, that they have long been associated with divination. In Cicero's *De Divinatione*, the statesman—himself an augur—relates that while augury is a form of divination that requires skill or art, sleep is by contrast a natural form of divination.

The candle reading you'll learn about in this book would fall into Cicero's first category of divination—it is an art which requires a certain amount of knowledge and skill to perform and interpret.

Yet there's no doubt that you can sharpen your skills by also being more aware of your dreams, by reflecting on them and on what they may be trying to tell you.

If you think about it for a moment, I'm sure you can come up with a particularly prophetic dream that you've had. Or maybe you're that lucky breed who has such dreams all the time.

Prophetic dreams tend to be very emotional experiences and we often attribute great meaning and purpose to them.

It is said that the Vestal Rhea Silvia dreamt of her son's greatness in the form of a palm tree that grew to reach the sky and cover the world. Similarly, Olympias, the mother of Alexander the Great, dreamt that a thunderbolt struck her womb and kindled a great fire, thus foretelling her son's power. Atia, the mother of Caesar Augustus, dreamt while she was pregnant that her vitals were carried to the stars and spread out over the world, thus prophesizing her son's rise to greatness. Augustus often used this prophetic dream (among many others!) to suggest divine validation for his rule.

There is no doubt that intense or strangely prophetic dreams during pregnancy are very common. I was about six months into my pregnancy when I dreamt that my son (I didn't know his gender at the time) looked like a tiny, hamster-sized doll. In the dream, he crawled up my arm (the same way a hamster does, if you've ever had one). I plucked him off my arm and set him on a blanket, afraid to touch him because he was so small. My mother appeared at my shoulder and said, "Don't be scared to touch your own child."

Well, as it happened, my son was born via emergency Caesarean section only a few weeks later, at the beginning of my seventh month of pregnancy. He was two full months premature and weighed only a kilogram (about two pounds). For the next two months, I lived with him in the hospital, many times having to summon the courage to touch him.

Not only was I terrified to hurt his tissue-thin red skin, but the tubes and sensors on his little body were scary to navigate. Many times I thought back to that dream and my mom's advice: "Don't be scared to touch your own child." That dream definitely gave me the confidence to touch him, to connect with him and care for him. (He's all grown up now and perfectly healthy, by the way!).

These kinds of prophetic or purposeful dreams often occur during times of high emotion or life transitions, whether it's pregnancy, a midlife crisis, relocation, a death or divorce, and so on.

As much as these dreams are or may seem prophetic, they are also intuitive. It's like our dreams have little roots that extend into our deepest thoughts and emotions, into the very energy of our being, and then spout up in the form of a dream that makes us sit up in bed and exclaim, "Wow, that *must* mean something!"

Of course it does! So if you have such dreams, write them down immediately. Keep track of them. Explore their meaning or their message and then remember that as you perform your candle reading. This will ensure all of your intuitive powers are engaged.

Fighting Fear

Fear can be a good thing. It can motivate us to take care of ourselves. It's like anger—it may seem like a bad emotion, but if considered wisely and measuredly, it can be a good thing. Much good has come about because we have been afraid of something.

The situation isn't so good, however, when fear starts to run the show. When it overwhelms us, confuses us, controls us, or takes away our liberty so that it starts making our life decisions for us.

You can't go back to school at your age...everyone will laugh at you.

You'll never find someone to love and who will love you back...so stop trying.

Don't take that trip—the plane might crash!

When it comes to candle reading, I want you to think about the questions you want to divine or discover the answers to. Is fear prompting you to ask them? Or are you asking them of your own accord, as a healthy and secure person who is just seeking answers?

I'm not saying that fear won't or shouldn't factor into the questions you ask. But it should be healthy fear, not crippling fear.

If you you're looking for an answer to the question, "Should I buy this house or is it too old?" and you have underlying fears about the strange smell in the basement...well, that's a healthy fear!

If you're looking for an answer to the question, "Should I go on this date?" and you're overwhelmed by visions of your date laughing at you, thinking you're unattractive or uninteresting...well, that's an unhealthy fear.

Learn to recognize the difference. Appreciate your healthy fear and work with it. But also have the courage to face your unhealthy fear and call it what it is—a liar.

Because unhealthy fear is a masterful and compulsive liar. It comes, ghost-like, in the dark, to whisper all kinds of lies into a person's ear—you're too old, you're unattractive, you'll never be happy, you've wasted your life, you're not successful enough…and on and on.

But if you can turn on the lights and look at it, if you can see it clearly, you will realize that it isn't as scary as you think. It's like looking at a terrifying figure in a dark corner of your bedroom, then flicking on the light and realizing it's just your housecoat.

I encourage you to identify your unhealthy fears (the lies) and then challenge the assumptions you are making that are sustaining them. Pick each fear apart, piece by piece, until it falls apart. If you can compel yourself to do it once, you'll build the confidence and courage you need to keep doing it. You can start with something small, and work your way up to the big things.

You can silence the liar. And once you do, you will be free to see your truths a lot more clearly.

In antiquity, the Eleusinian Mysteries were a form of religious rites that were highly secretive. It was said that those initiated in the Eleusinian rites obtained such a strong certainty of the afterlife, and such confidence in the truth of the eternal cycle, that they lost their fear of death.

It is my hope that candle reading with Vesta's eternal flame will bring you not just answers, but also the kind of comfort that can help you put many fears to rest.

Finding Peace

When it comes right down to it, what are we looking for when we do a candle reading, or any kind of divination for that matter? We're looking for answers, yes. But more than that, I think we're often looking for reassurance. For peace.

We want to know that everything is going to be all right.

That's why the ancient Romans were so diligent about the rites and rituals they performed in honor of their gods. They wanted to maintain the pax deorum, the peaceful accord that humankind had with the gods.

It's why the Vestals tended so diligently and so religiously to the sacred fire in the temple, reading the flames to ensure they remained in the goddess's favor.

Vesta is a protective goddess. She was *the* protective goddess of Rome. She was honored grandly in her temple and modestly in every home because, like us, the ancients wanted to know that everything was going to be all right.

You want to know it too.

If you can be clear about the questions you want to discover or divine the answers to, if you can be reasonably free of fear and full of peace, and if you can learn to truly listen to your own intuition, you will be rewarded with a candle reading that not only sheds light on your life, but brings peace to it as well.

And what greater purpose could divination serve than that?

*This world, which is the same for all,
has not been made by any god or man,
but it always has been, is, and will be
an ever-living fire.*

- Heraclitus, Greek Philosopher, 544-484 BCE

CHAPTER THREE

Divination Candles

I know you want to dive into candle divination, but let's take a few minutes to look at the different candles you can use. You have more options than you think, and choosing this or that candle can have dramatic effects on your experience of the ritual. The type of candle you choose to nourish Vesta's flame is important!

Beeswax Candles

Although you can use almost any type of candle wax for divination purposes, beeswax candles can be particularly useful. This is because of the unique qualities that pure beeswax possesses.

Pure amber beeswax—unbleached, undyed, and not cut with cheaper waxes such as soy or paraffin—does two things that are of extreme importance when it comes to divination.

First, burning pure beeswax releases negative ions into the air, which in turn purifies the air of toxins and allergens. Since Vesta is a purifying spirit, and because the ancients always purified their sacrifices or offerings to the gods and to her, that is very useful.

Burning beeswax can therefore create the kind of pure aura, literally and metaphorically, that facilitates the ritual.

Second, burning beeswax releases a certain fragrance that is believed to stimulate the pituitary gland at the base of the brain, which in turn stimulates and enhances intuition.

Intuition is a very important component of candle reading, especially when it comes time to interpret the signs you have been given. In the chapter on interpretation, I will present you with an inventory of signs and symbols that will help you read your candle; however, there is definitely a personal, subjective aspect to doing this. The more your intuition can be engaged, the better you will be able to interpret the signs and the more meaning you will find in your overall reading.

In fact, if you are pondering a particularly important or emotional life question, I recommend that you consider using a beeswax candle, particularly one that is a) pure beeswax, unbleached and uncut with other wax types; b) has a wood wick, and; c) is either circular in shape or housed in a circular clear or white container.

When purchasing a beeswax candle, make sure the wax is 100% pure beeswax. Beware labels: they may say "100% beeswax" but that may only pertain to the 5% portion of the overall wax blend that is made of beeswax! It's a dodgy but common labeling practice.

Instead, specifically enquire as to whether there are other waxes present in the candle. You will require pure beeswax in your candle to best enhance intuition.

Also, be good to the bees! There is a worldwide decline in the honeybee population, which makes it important to only purchase beeswax candles from ethical sources.

In antiquity, the Romans believed that when the fire crackled, popped, hissed or snapped, Vesta was speaking to them. That is why using a candle with a wood wick—which similarly crackles as it burns—is a wonderful idea. Listening—observing—for signs in the crackles of the wick can thus bring an extra dimension to candle divination with beeswax, the type of wax the ancient Romans used most often (along with tallow, a rendered form of animal fat).

When it comes to candle divination, my preference—again, especially if you have more serious or emotional questions to ask— is to burn a circular pillar or taper candle, or a candle housed within a circular container (as opposed to a molded shape candle).

This pays tribute to the round firebowl the sacred fire was kept in, as well as the circular shape of the temple itself. The temple was made of white marble, so you may wish to choose a white container, although clear glass—to admire and read the melting amber beeswax and the flame—is also a great choice.

While beeswax candles can be incredibly powerful and useful for candle divination, they do present one little problem. Because beeswax has a very high melting point—higher than soy and paraffin—beeswax candles don't tend to drip as much as other candle wax types. They also burn slower, which can be an issue if you're looking for a quick reading.

When we get to the chapter on interpreting signs, you'll see that one thing we look for is waxicles—those long wax trails that run down the surface of candles as the wax melts. You'll definitely see more of these and other formations with non-beeswax candles than you will with beeswax candles.

There are ways to compensate for the limitations of beeswax, though. The most obvious and beneficial way is to focus more on reading the flame and vapor of a beeswax candle, as well as on the sounds from a wood wick. Those are incredibly important readings that are just as significant and meaningful as wax readings. After all, the goddess is in the flame.

Indeed, there one extremely compelling reason to use pure beeswax for flame-focused readings. Because beeswax burns at such a high temperature, it emits light that is similar to sunlight in terms of the light spectrum.

Vesta's sacred flame is associated with sunlight in various ways. The doors of her temple faced east, toward the rising sun. The annual renewal ceremony, which involved re-lighting her sacred flame, may have used sunbeams as a source of ignition.

Accordingly, even a beeswax tealight can produce a divine, sun-like flame for you to admire, one that releases a delightful beeswax fragrance and lets you perform a reading in a relatively short period of time. And if you can find one with a wood wick, all the better!

Yet don't assume from this discussion that beeswax candles are only good for reading the flame. There will almost always be some wax changes to read with a beeswax candle. You may also see more waxicles and wax activity with thinner beeswax candles, such as tapers, or with candles that are molded or sculpted and which may melt in more curious ways.

The manufacture and composition of a particular beeswax candle will also affect how it burns and what formations you see within the parameters of your ritual. The flame is a living thing and every burn is unique. So you just never know…

Another option is to do the opposite of what I've told you—that is, to purchase a beeswax candle that is cut with soy or other more drippy wax types. In this case, the less beeswax the better! You may still get some benefit of enhanced intuition, while also seeing more drips and distinctive wax signs.

Soy Candles

Soy wax is made from soybean oil and is often found in container candles, most likely because it has a much lower melting point than beeswax. When in a pillar or molded candle, it is often blended with another wax type. Soy candles are widely available, less expensive than beeswax, and are relatively easy to find with wood wicks that snap and crackle just as well in soy wax as they do in beeswax.

Soy wax is naturally white, which is a lovely way to pay tribute to the white marble of Vesta's temple and the white dresses of her priestesses.

Soy wax candles make a nice alternative or adjunct to beeswax and you can certainly use them for candle divination, regardless of whether they're in pillar form, in a specialty shape or in a container. And if you choose one with a wood wick, you'll most likely be treated to a great opportunity to hear the voice of Vesta.

You may also find that many designer and luxury candles are made of soy. These are an indulgence, to be sure, but if your budget permits such indulgences, there's no reason not to treat yourself. After all, Vesta's priestesses lived lives of prestige and luxury.

While soy candles may not burn with a flame quite as lovely as beeswax ones, the flame you will see from a soy candle is nonetheless extremely beautiful. It tends to be soft and natural, and can really draw you in. Plus, soy is biodegradable, easy to clean, non-toxic, and doesn't produce soot.

Paraffin Candles

Paraffin wax is made from petroleum, a by-product of refining crude oil. While some research suggests burning paraffin candles releases toxic chemicals, it also seems the amounts involved in casual candle use is far too small to be harmful to healthy people.

Regardless, paraffin remains the most used, most versatile and least expensive wax in the world, and it is used to make everything from cheap emergency-use candles to costly designer beauties with customized fragrances.

Paraffin candles come in all shapes from pillars to novelty, and hold color and scent really well. Paraffin is often blended with other wax types to improve or tailor a candle's performance.

Personally, I do burn paraffin wax candles now and then. A paraffin pillar candle—because it burns so hot (it has a low melting point) and fast—can result in an abundant variety of interesting waxicles and wax activity that can facilitate a fantastic reading. And once in a while I'll spot a paraffin candle in a meaningful or unusual shape, and I'll get curious as to what kind of reading will result.

Recently, a good friend showed up for coffee. She had picked up some sweets for us at the local farmers' market, but had also purchased a large and strikingly colored hand-sculpted paraffin candle. She was determined to use it for a candle reading, even though it was quite expensive.

So we did a reading. It didn't take too long and we didn't have to burn too much of the candle before we were rewarded with more than enough interesting signs to read: waxicles, shapes, slopes, a spike or two, and even a little wax pool.

In fact, after we extinguished the candle and interpreted the signs, thus completing her reading, she was even more pleased with the appearance of her candle.

The divination ritual had resulted in an even more interestingly shaped candle. And since her reading was a very favorable one, she kept the candle as a keepsake, vowing to never light it again. It now sits on her bookshelf.

Palm Candles

Like soy wax, palm wax is natural, clean-burning, has a high melting point, and results in beautifully textured candles. Like all the waxes mentioned here, it may be blended with other waxes to change its properties and make it more or less suitable for certain candle types. Yet palm wax has its critics. It is made from the fruit of palm oil trees in South America and South Asia, and has been associated with deforestation. The same problems can arise with soy wax, as it is also plant-based. Yet there are definitely ethical and eco-friendly sellers out there, and with a little research, you'll find them!

Other Candle Waxes

While I've covered some common and widely available wax types here, as with anything else, innovation is a constant and there will always be new or specialty products coming out.

Coconut wax, made from coconut oil, is a really interesting option: it may be blended with something like soy or beeswax to improve its performance, can be found with wood wicks, and is typically seen in container candles. Rapeseed wax, also called canola oil wax, comes from canola and is another natural option.

More and more, we are seeing a candle industry that is trying to be health conscious, vegan, and sustainable while also innovating to create beautiful, unique candles in the process. That goes for small artisan shops and larger companies. All waxes have their pros and cons, and I'm not steering you toward one "best" type (although personally, I steer clear of dripless and gel candles for divination). I only encourage you to put conscious thought into the wax types and blends you use, because this will factor into your readings. The divination methodology you'll learn here can be applied to all wax types, including new ones that enter the market, so experiment!

In fact, you'll want to change things up by deliberately choosing the wax types or blends that complement and best align with your particular mood, purpose or time schedule.

A relatively short, fast paraffin burn might be ideal for a quick, fun reading with friends. Or if you're doing your candle reading alone and are looking for "big" signs, then a paraffin candle's comparatively dramatic melting process might be perfect.

On the contrary, a long, slow beeswax burn might be needed for those more introspective readings, when you need input from your intuition and you want to focus on Vesta's sun-like flame.

An exotic coconut wax or luxury soy blend might add something special to those times you want to indulge yourself in stronger fragrance or the crackle of the flame on a wood wick.

Variety is the spice of life. And remember, as with any other consumer product, you have the power. As I said when I discussed beeswax, I encourage you to do your homework and always purchase from ethical sources. Many companies see the benefit of selling eco-friendly candles, so they are not hard to find these days.

The Architecture of a Candle

Now that you're familiar with various candle wax types, and before we get into the specifics of a candle divination reading, let's take a moment to identify the parts of a candle. This may seem pedantic, but when it comes time to observe the signs, you'll need an accurate way to read and record their positions on the candle.

While you can use a variety of candle types for divination, pillar and taper candles are arguably the most common. And since these resemble an ancient column, I've borrowed from the architectural elements of columns to identify the parts of a candle.

The capital. The capital is the top portion of the candle, which includes the exposed wick.

The column. The column is the outside surface of the candle, whether circular (as with a pillar or taper) or another shape.

The base. The base is the bottom of the candle. If wax drips down the column of a candle to pool around the bottom, and if it pools on the tray, surface, or holder the candle is sitting on, the base of the candle is understood to include this wax pool.

Container Candles

This architecture of a candle can be applied to almost any style or shape, since all candles burn top to bottom (obviously!).

The top (including the exposed wick) will always be the capital, the middle will always be the column, and the bottom will always be the base. This applies to candles in containers too, whether it's a short votive in a jar or a tall candle set into a narrow glass religious container.

While I've said that clear glass and white containers are both great choices because they pay tribute to the round, white Temple of Vesta, clear glass containers do make container candle divinations easier, as you can more clearly read the wax within and on the sides.

I'd also like to mention that tealights, if left in the cup, are considered container candles. Happily, you can now find them in clear plastic cups rather than those cheap little metal ones. This makes them prettier while also making it easier to read the wax.

Molded Candles

Molded candles—those poured into the shape of anything from trees to turtles and sparrows to superheroes—abound. You can't turn around in a gift shop without knocking a few over.

But don't make the mistake of thinking they're all cutesy or novelty items. There are some gorgeous ones out there. I recently saw a line of shapely, sophisticated candles molded into the graceful shapes of famous statues, including Venus bathing.

The good thing about these candles is that many are quite small and most have a variety of curves, peaks and valleys for the melting wax to travel: depending on the wax type and manufacture, this can result in relatively quick readings and high-interest signs.

As importantly, the variety of size and subject matter available with molded candles gives you the option to burn a shape that has symbolic meaning to you in a personal sense, or that complements that type of question you are seeking an answer to.

For example, a woman I knew who recently lost her mother said that she burned a candle that was in the shape of a starfish. She chose this because one of her favorite childhood memories was walking along the beach with her mother and finding starfish.

When she read her candle, she found that the smooth slides of wax that formed on the left-hand side were comforting to her, as she took them as a sign her mother would want to soothe her.

Not too long ago, I had a friend who turned sixty. To mark the occasion, we put a candle molded into a "60" onto her cake, and let it burn for a while before she extinguished it.

When it came time to interpret the signs, we found, among other things, that the 6 (situated to the left) had barely melted at all while the 0 had basically deteriorated into a sloppy, melted mess. The steadfast 6 was a sign of strength and a welcome birthday gift, one that had an uplifting emotional impact on her.

You can also choose a subject matter or symbol that meant something to the ancients who most fervently honored Vesta. A shell, for example, is one symbol of Venus, the goddess of love.

When a good friend of mine had reservations about a man she had started to date, I suggested she use a shell candle in her divination ritual. She did, and reported that her reading confirmed what she intuitively knew to be true—he was bad news.

You can do something similar. If you're looking for signs of wisdom or need a wise answer to something, burn an owl candle: the owl is the animal of Minerva, goddess of wisdom.

If you're looking for signs of strength or inspiration to endure or win an upcoming conflict of some kind, burn a candle in the shape of a wolf: the wolf is the animal of Mars, god of war. After all, life has its share of battles and sometimes there's no avoiding them.

The ancient Romans loved their symbols. When you reach the chapter on interpretation, you'll find a list of these, along with their meanings in antiquity and in modern candle divination.

Hand-Carved & Specialty Candles

I mention hand-carved and specialty candles under their own heading here for a couple reasons. Hand-carved candles are often fairly large and expensive, and many are one-of-a-kind works of art that took great expertise to craft.

They are a wonderful choice if you want to treat yourself to a particularly bold and beautiful burn, or if you are trying to bring more beauty into your life and your candle reading.

Dedicating a luxury or chic candle to Vesta's flame is a fitting offering. In fact, the ornate scrolls often seen on hand-carved candles remind me of the scrolls on an Ionic column, the kind of column that once adorned the Temple of Vesta.

I've seen other hand-carved candles that have been sculpted with flowers on their sides. This can symbolize a fresh start or new beginning, and are a suitable choice if you're in that frame of mind.

Like my friend who burned part of her sculpted candle and then kept the rest as a keepsake, you may also want to do the same. Depending on the wax type and formation, these candles often show interesting and usable signs in a relatively short time, so it's unnecessary to burn them too far down.

Rather, you may want to save them as an ornament and an artistic, unique memento of your reading, especially if it was a particularly favorable, meaningful or inspiring one.

Turning to specialty candles: by specialty, I mean candles, often made by artisans, which may have extra materials in the wax, such as flowers petals or herbs. There is no doubt these can also be gorgeous works of art—I only encourage you to double-check their safe usage with the candle-maker or follow their burn instructions carefully. Like sculpted candles, they too can make great mementos.

In fact, when a friend of mine opened a coffee shop, I gifted her with a beautiful specialty candle with coffee beans in the wax. We used it for a really productive reading and, when it was over, she displayed it in her coffee shop as a good luck charm.

My point in all of this is to encourage you to think creatively and whenever possible—especially for special or important occasions—consider burning a candle whose special beauty or tailored symbolism can add extra meaning to your candle divination.

DIY Candles

Every March 1st, in honor of the day that the Vestals renewed the sacred fire in the temple, I create my own small batch of hand-poured beeswax candles with wood wicks.

To be absolutely certain that I'm using pure beeswax, I collect honeycomb cappings from a local apiary and render them into wax myself, performing the whole messy, time-consuming, but satisfying process as a sort of personal ritual.

I only use these candles in especially important divinations for myself, family or close friends—those times and burns where I really want to focus on reading the flame with the benefit of intuition-enhancing beeswax.

I love to see the reflection of the flame against the glass and within the pool of amber beeswax as it melts in the glass container. Depending on where and how the wax builds up against the sides of the container, I'll take it as a favorable or unfavorable sign.

I hope this chapter has shown you that there are more than enough meaningful ways to use a purchased candle for your readings. You don't have to make your own. Most of the time, it just isn't worth the trouble! Personally, I like the ease and variety of purchasing candles, whether from the grocery store or a true artisan.

Nonetheless, if you find that you really take to candle divination and you'd like to create your own candles, do it! There are many excellent resources and books out there that can help you learn how to do this in a safe, creative and meaningful way.

Wick Types

A candle wick isn't the kind of thing that most people put a lot of thought into. Yet it too is a consideration when it comes to candle divination. After all, it is the wick that burns with Vesta's fire and delivers nourishment, in the form of candle wax, to the flame.

You already know about my affection for wood wicks and why I feel the way I do. Happily, wood wicks are widely available in various candle styles and wax blends, so you shouldn't have any trouble finding one that you love and that will suit your purpose.

In addition to the beautiful crackle of a wood wick and the ability to look and listen for signs in the sound, wood is of course the most natural, authentic, and ancient material used to nourish Vesta's flame. No doubt that is why she speaks so clearly through it.

That being said, cotton wicks are perfectly acceptable: flat or knitted wicks are very common, especially in pillar candles or taper candles, while square wicks are often used in beeswax as they burn a little stronger.

Yet when it comes to fiber wicks and candle divination, my personal preference is to avoid wicks that are cored with metal, such as zinc. While a cored wick can do a nice job of keeping the wick straight, there's just something unnatural about having the flame burn on a metal core. If you can, try to choose wicks that are cored with cotton or paper. It just seems more natural, doesn't it?

And just a word about multi-wick candles. While I love these, especially when the wicks are made of wood, they aren't suitable for candle reading. There's just too much going on. As you'll see, the protocols for lighting and extinguishing the flame, for observing and interpreting the signs—it's just not possible when there's more than one flame burning. So save these beauties for other occasions, and stick to single-wick candles for divination.

The Most Important Things…

Safety is one of them. As I end this chapter, I will remind you of the obvious. Always follow the candle manufacturer's safety recommendations, keep an eye on things, and use common sense. The divination practices I present here are my own. If you need to modify them for safety reasons, then do. Respect the power of fire.

Which leads me to the second important thing I want to mention—having respect for the flame that burns on your candle in a deeper sense, since that point of living light and heat is the goddess herself. It doesn't matter if you're burning a candle from a luxury designer or the dollar store, once you call upon the goddess to enter it, once you light her flame, she is with you. Just as she was with the Vestal Virgins in days gone by, just as she was with the Caesars and millions of other people throughout the centuries, she is with you.

The first Vestal candle I burned in my life was given to me at the ruins of the Temple of Vesta in the Roman Forum when I was twenty years old. Hand-poured beeswax in a white glass container, I have no doubt the elderly woman who gifted it to me—thus sparking a lifelong interest in all things Vesta—had many times called Vesta to enter it. Decades later, I still have it, though I only light it once a year—every March 1st, so I can add a drop of its melted wax to my own batch of Vestal candles. Each time I do so, I am struck by the greatness of the goddess, past and present, and my respect for her is renewed. If you respect the flame you hold in your hands, I know that you too will feel that sense of reverence and Vesta's presence.

*To thy hands, Troy entrusts
her holy things and household gods,
and Vesta's ever-bright, undying fire.*

- Virgil, Roman Poet, 70-19 BCE

CHAPTER FOUR

Candle Divination:
Methodology & Procedure

Vesta's *flamma* & Divination

As I said back in chapter one, I have merged the past and the present to create a modern system of candle reading divination that reflects and respects the goddess of fire, Vesta. That's why I've borrowed elements and terminology from the ancient practice of augury (among other things, which you'll read about as we go on).

Augury would have been very familiar to the priestesses of Vesta, those women who dutifully cared for her flame in the temple and intimately knew her fiery voice. Augury was a fundamental part of the Vestals' religious worldview, and in addition to reading the sacred fire in the temple, it was a primary way they and their fellow Romans asked for and received signs from the gods.

In this chapter, I will go into more detail about how the Vesta method of candle divination works, including how it utilizes and adapts certain elements of augury to receive and read the signs from Vesta's *flamma* in a practical and usable way.

The Divination Grid: The Templum

You'll recall that taking the auspices involved an augur using a staff to mark out a section of the sky called the templum: the observing of signs would then take place within this sacred space.

For our purposes, the templum can be understood as an imaginary grid the augur would position over the sky, thus dividing it into quadrants. This made it easier to observe and precisely record where and what kinds of signs appeared in the heavens.

I envisioned that the Vestals may have used a similar imaginary grid over the round firebowl that contained Vesta's fire to observe and precisely record where and what kinds of signs appeared in the sacred fire.

In the same way, if you look down at the top of a round candle from above, you can envision a similar imaginary grid over it, dividing it into four equal (pie-shaped) quadrants, with the wick positioned in the center of the grid.

This is the candle's templum, and it is within these four quadrants, from above, that you will observe and precisely record the signs on all parts of the candle, so that you can interpret them later.

The templum has four directions: antica (forward-facing), postica (rear-facing), sinistra (the left), and dextera (the right).

This means that if you were to read your candle when facing east, you would look down at your candle from above and imagine the capital as the face of a clock: the 12 o'clock position would be facing forward, or antica:

Although I've used a round candle here—it could be a pillar candle or a taper candle—this basic divination grid, or templum, can be applied and adapted to a variety of candle styles and sizes, including irregular ones such as molded shape candles.

The establishing point will always be the wick—the flame of Vesta—which will be at the center of the grid, and that portion of the candle within the templum will be observed for signs. In this example of a turtle-shaped candle, the grid is centered over the wick:

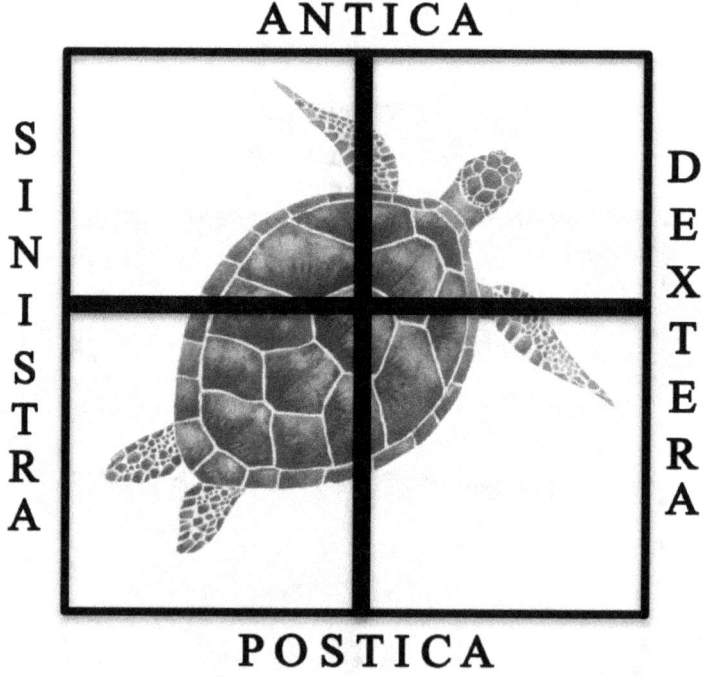

ANTICA

SINISTRA

DEXTERA

POSTICA

It's fine if the quadrants of the grid contain unequal amounts of wax or irregular parts of the candle; however, in such cases, it is helpful to take a photo of the candle before you begin the burn, so that you can remember its original shape when it comes time to observe the melted wax and record the signs.

Another option with irregular and/or large-sized candles is to mark off a templum that only includes a select or smaller portion of the entire candle, as shown below.

You will then only observe and record signs from the area inside the templum.

This decision, whether to position the whole candle within the templum (which is the standard practice) or to mark off a portion of it for the templum, is your choice when it comes to irregular and/or larger candles (or any candle, for that matter).

Just remember that the templum should be marked off from a position of looking down at the candle from above (as the Vestals would have looked down at the sacred fire), with the wick in the center of the divination grid.

ANTICA

S
I
N
I
S
T
R
A

D
E
X
T
E
R
A

POSTICA

Regardless of what type of non-container candle you are burning—pillar, taper, molded or hand-carved—and depending on how long your reading lasts and what type of wax your candle is made of, you may see wax pool at the base of your candle.

In such cases, the general rule remains: the grid should be positioned with the wick in its center. This is true even if the position of the candle and/or the wick slopes or shifts during the burn: use the shifted position of the wick to re-center the divination grid before you do record the signs. As with many things I'll cover in this chapter, this will make more sense as we move on.

ANTICA

SINISTRA

DEXTERA

POSTICA

Establishing the Finis

Whereas the templum is the prescribed area of the candle within which you will read the signs, the *finis* is the designated larger area around it, the area that establishes the boundaries of the ritual as a whole. The finis will include your candle, as well as all your divination tools and supplies.

The ancients typically used stone markers called *termini* to establish such boundaries, and you can do the same. I recommend you find four beautiful stones—anywhere from the size of a plum to the size of an apple—that you can use to mark off the square or rectangular boundary of the divination ritual.

Because the Romans tended to make such things on the fancy side, you may wish to do the same. You can purchase fine polished stones, or polish your own findings. Crystals are fine, as are stones with words engraved on them, or shaped into animals or figures.

Another option is to use statuettes of the gods and goddesses to mark off the templum. They can pull double duty as handsome home décor when you are not divining.

Once you have set the termini at the four corners of the finis boundaries, you will need to purify the space. You can do this by sprinkling a bit of salt—a purifying element—whether from a shaker or your hand, over the surface of the finis.

In practice, you will establish the finis before you mark off the templum; however, I thought it would make more sense to give you a solid understanding of the templum first, so that's what I did.

Regardless, you can see the Latin word finis in the word definition, which is what we're doing when we mark off a finis—we're defining the boundaries of our candle divination ritual as a whole.

Primary & Secondary Orientations

In chapter one, when I gave a very general description of the practice of ancient augury, I said that the augur faced south or sometimes east when marking out the templum. In the diagram of the circular candle I presented earlier in this chapter when discussing the templum, I indicated an east-facing direction.

In antiquity, the direction or orientation may have changed or a least been different depending on why the auspices were being taken, what they were meant to determine, or who was taking them and on whose behalf. Were they being taken by an augur on behalf of the emperor to determine the ideal date to go to war? Were they being taken by a priest-for-hire on behalf of a private citizen to determine whether his daughter should marry Lucius or Gaius? The system for taking the auspices may also have gone through reforms. Moreover, we know that augury was practiced by the Etruscans and the Greeks, and no doubt those protocols factored into the distinct way that the Romans would ultimately take the auspices. So augury was complex and varied.

Yet when it came to orientation, regardless of whether the augur faced south or east, the left-hand side continued to be favorable, at least as a general rule. This is important to remember.

When facing east, the north was to the augur's left: you'll recall the ancients believed that the gods and goddesses lived in the northern part of the heavens. So signs in that region were good ones.

When facing south, the east was on the left: since the sun rises on the east, this direction was also considered favorable or fortunate. So signs in that region were also good ones.

In my method of candle wax divination, I've chosen the east-facing orientation as the primary one, since I believe this most closely aligns with the way the Vestals would have done it.

Accordingly, you will face the eastern direction first when performing a candle divination ritual in your home. The "first burn" will always be an east-facing one, so that signs which appear on your left, to the north, are favorable or significant. Signs which appear on your right, to the south, are less favorable or less significant.

If you choose to do a "second burn"—perhaps the signs were unclear or you just want to compare and contrast the signs you receive—you can then move on to the secondary orientation, which is south facing, to perform the second reading.

In the secondary south-facing orientation, signs which appear on your left, to the east, are favorable or significant. Signs which appear on your right, to the west, are less favorable or less significant.

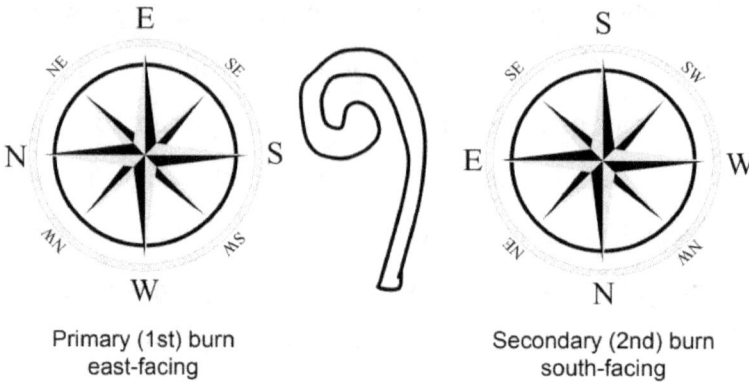

Primary (1st) burn
east-facing

Secondary (2nd) burn
south-facing

A few more words about orientation and first and second burns: if you do decide to perform a second burn in the secondary south-facing direction, you must wait until the entire divination ritual for the primary east-facing burn has been completed.

You must also use a new candle and start the entire ritual again, from the beginning. You cannot simply pivot in your chair to face south and keep going with the same candle.

Each orientation and burn should be considered its own complete and unique reading.

Again, it isn't required that you perform two readings. Yet if you have the time and the inclination, it can be insightful to compare and contrast the signs received in each. This is particularly true if you add some variety to the candle types or waxes you use, as well as which divination rituals you perform.

For example, it can be interesting to compare the reading from a beeswax taper candle in the primary east orientation with the reading from a molded paraffin candle in the secondary south orientation.

In the same way, you might choose a thick pillar candle to perform a fairly lengthy reading in the primary east orientation, but then complement that by performing a wax drippings in water reading (that chapter is coming up soon!) in the secondary south orientation. Because a wax drippings in water reading can be completed more quickly, and can deliver very dramatic and distinct signs, this is a great combination of readings.

Other Divination Tools

While your candle—and its size, shape, style, and wax type or wax blend—is of course your primary divination tool, you will need a few other supplies to perform a candle reading.

• Divination grids. You will need a number of either printed or hand-drawn divination grids of the four-square grid template used to observe and record the signs from the burn.

These should be large enough that you can make a few notes in each quadrant to record what you are seeing in that quadrant of the candle, or even draw a few shapes to record what you are seeing.

If you hand-draw your divination grid, be sure to use a ruler so that each quadrant is equal. Your grid paper should also include what orientation the burn was taken in, whether primary or secondary.

• A record book or journal. The priests and priestesses of ancient Rome, including the Vestals, kept meticulous religious records to document the details of each ritual, as well as the signs they saw from the gods.

The famous Sibylline Books, for example, contained the *fata deorum*—the words or prophecies of the gods. During times of need or uncertainty, a passage would be selected at random and a priest would interpret it, thus divining the will or advice of the gods.

It's important that you do a similar thing. Keep a record, journal, or book, of the signs that you see during each and every candle divination you perform. Ever.

These records should include the date, time, and location of the burn, the orientation(s), a description of the candle, wick type, and candle wax (you can include a picture or drawing if you wish), and a description of the templum.

These records should also include a detailed account of each and every ritual, from invoking to the goddess to your observations of the signs and your final interpretation of them (more on all of this in the next heading). You should store the divination grids of each reading in this book or journal. Don't throw anything away.

In this way, you can look back on previous readings during times of need or uncertainty. You can also use information from past readings to help you better understand the trend of your readings, put them in context, or understand a particularly cryptic reading.

• Wood matches. Because the Vestals' most common method of renewing the sacred fire was likely wood friction (they used the branches of a sacred oak tree, called the *arbor felix*), it is important that the flame used in candle divination is ignited with a wood match. I believe this is the most natural way to invoke Vesta's spirit.

• A compass. You must have your orientation—east or south—correct. You should therefore use a compass to establish it.

• Four termini. These will mark the boundaries of the finis.

• Salt. You will use this to purify the area of the finis. You only need a little, so a few shakes of a salt shaker will do.

• A candle snuffer. When it is time to extinguish the flame, it's essential that you don't blow on it. Not only is this fairly graceless, but it may cause tiny wax droplets to splatter and thus corrupt your reading. Blowing on a candle also unduly influences the resultant smoke from extinguishment, thus making a vapor reading unusable. Instead, use a candle snuffer.

• A little lituus. Just as the augur used a staff to mark out the templum, you'll need to mark out your templum on your candle. To do this, I actually use an ancient Roman iron striker that has a scroll on one end, similar to the curve in an augur's staff.

To me, this has a nice association with fire and Vesta. However, I usually recommend that people simply use the straight handle of their candle snuffer. It does a great job and its association with fire gives it meaning.

• An offering or libation to Vesta. In antiquity, offerings of bread or salted flour, or libations of olive oil, milk, or wine, were tossed into the hearthfire or sprinkled into the flame of a candle at mealtime to honor Vesta.

Today, those who honor Vesta often leave an earthenware bowl of offerings and/or libations by her flame as a symbolic offering or libation. You should do the same.

Although you can choose whatever vessels you wish to house your offerings or libations, one of my favorite ways to do this is to use a fine or vintage teacup and saucer: I place a little fresh oil into the cup, and then I add some freshly-salted flour to the saucer. I often use a cup and saucer from a set my grandmother left me.

Another option here is to create a simplified version of the type of sacred wafer that the Vestal Virgins used to bake. These were used to symbolically purify sacrificial animals and were also a traditional offering into the sacred fire.

To do this, simply mix flour, water, and salt together, shape into thin round wafers, and bake on a tray in the oven for a few moments. These hardened wafers can then be safely passed over the flame of your divination candle as an offering to Vesta.

(Incidentally, if these sacred wafers remind you of communion wafers, it is because the Catholic nuns took them directly from the Vestal priestesses.)

The last thing I'd like to mention in this section isn't really a divination tool or supply, but nonetheless it is something to consider. And that is location. Where will you perform the candle divination ritual? On a table? On a window sill?

As long as you're facing in the proper direction (east or south), and as long as you've designated an ideal setting for the finis, one where you can properly position your four termini and sprinkle salt to purify the space, the location doesn't really matter. It's up to you. You can even vary the location if you want from this ritual to the next.

The divination ritual can also be performed outdoors if it's a breezeless and temperate day.

Another option is to perform the ritual on your household shrine. In antiquity, each home had a *lararium.* This was a family shrine or altar that held images of the household gods and a candle or oil lamp that burned with Vesta's sacred flame. You can think of it as a private or domestic version of a sacred altar in a temple.

A modern lararium can be almost anything. It can be a marble table or a wooden temple-shaped structure, a trendy wine cart or a vintage entrance cabinet. It can even be a shelf. Many homes have architectural elements—like a recessed wall niche—that can also work. Ideally, it is located near the home's main entrance.

You can adorn your lararium as you wish, with candles, meaningful items, and fresh flowers or laurel: in fact, the Temple of Vesta was often decorated with laurel and I like to place fragrant bay (laurel) leaves in a bowl on my lararium as an offering.

Yet don't feel tied to performing your candle reading on a lararium, or anywhere else. Vesta's spirit resides in the flame of the candle, so there is no particular spot you must perform the ritual in.

The Three Stages of Candle Divination

There are three general stages of a candle divination. These are *Invocatio*, *Spectio*, and *Coniectura*. I will discuss each in some detail now. I will also give you an idea of how each phase might look in practice.

1. *Invocatio*. The invocation stage is the first true stage of a candle divination ritual. It is when you will invoke or call upon Vesta to enter your candle and light the wick with her flame.

The invocatio stage is also when you will ask your specific question of Vesta, if you have one.

Before you perform the invocation, however, you must first ensure you are ready to do so by having done the following:

a) established the proper east or south orientation for the ritual, depending on whether this is a primary or secondary burn (if you're only doing one burn, you should face east);

b) established a finis within which to perform the ritual and sprinkled a bit of salt to purify the space;

c) set your offering or libation within the boundaries of the finis, and;

d) marked out the templum on your candle with the lituus, and taken photographs or made drawings of your pre-burn candle, if you wish to do so (in case you wish to compare these to the templum after the burn is complete).

To invoke the spirit of Vesta to enter your candle, you should say aloud:

"Visit this candle, Mother Vesta."

In Latin, this is *Invise hanc candelam, Mater Vesta.*

If you wish, and particularly if you are using a pillar candle, you can very lightly carve a V into the wax. This is optional, though.

Once you have said these words aloud—"Visit this candle, Mother Vesta" (or the Latin version)—you can light your wood match and hold it to the wick.

It's preferable to light the candle from the left. If you're facing east, as you should be in a primary burn, this will mean you are lighting the candle from the favorable north.

Hold the match's flame against the wick long enough for the flame to transfer to the wick and burn with a steady flame.

Once the flame is firmly established, say aloud:

"Vesta, if it be your will, send me an unmistakable sign within these boundaries that I have set."

Of course, the "boundaries" here refers to the templum and not the finis, as you will only observe for signs within the templum.

Now, you need to decide whether you want to ask a specific question or whether you are performing a general reading.

If you have a specific question, ask it aloud.

For example: "Will I find true love this year?" or "Should I accept the job offer I was just given?"

If you do not have a specific or yes/no question in mind, but are instead looking for a general reading that might reflect what is happening in your life, say aloud:

"Vesta, if it be your will, I await the signs."

To further establish the parameters of the ritual, you must indicate how long you will burn your candle. One hour? Two? Fifteen minutes? Regardless, this needs to be communicated. If you've decided on one hour, for example, you should say aloud:

"To receive the signs, I will burn your flame on this candle for one hour."

Although it is not necessary to do so, if you are going through a troubling time or want to emphasize something, or if you simply want to honor Vesta more deeply, you may wish to include an extra prayer to her during the invocatio stage.

The following prayers are inspired by ancient writings and you can certainly use them if you like.

Vesta, ancient and florid Mother,
let your blessing descend on me.
May your sacred fire burn for me
as always you made it burn for Rome.
Goddess, mother, guardian,
and fire that purifies and protects.
Protect me and my home and be kind to my
offering. Look at my affliction and if
you say so, my struggles will end.

The last sentence of this prayer, "Look at my affliction and if you say so, my struggles will end" can easily be amended to suit your personal situation and the purpose of your reading.

For example, you might say, "Look at my uncertainty and if you say so, my mind will be soothed."

Here is another:

> *Vesta, you dwell in my home*
> *with your everlasting fire,*
> *Eternal and ever-florid queen,*
> *laughing and blessed,*
> *Accept these rites.*

You can also speak your own words, perhaps beginning a prayer with this sentiment from the poet Ovid:

> *Vesta, favor me. I open my lips now in prayer,*
> *and ask to attend your sacred rites.*

2. *Spectio.* The spectio stage is the second stage in a candle divination ritual. This is when you will observe the signs in the flame, vapor (if you see any) and wax, as the candle burns. At this stage, you are a very invested spectator, thus the word spectio.

During this stage, you will sit quietly and watch the flame and candle in a state of reverent silence, or *silentium*. If you are burning beeswax, this is when your intuition can really be activated.

Although you won't record or interpret the signs in the candle wax until the flame has been extinguished and the wax has cooled and congealed, you should still write down your observations while the candle is burning.

For example, if you see any notable but perhaps transitory wax shifts, folds, slopes, drizzles or formations, make a note of where on the templum / divination grid they appeared: you can make these notes on the divination grid or in your journal.

As for the flame (as opposed to the wax), you must necessarily record its behavior and any signs in it during the spectio stage, while it is burning. So make sure you do that. Observe the flame and note in which direction / quadrants it tends to sway the most. Note whether it is tall and steady or short and sputtering. Note any unusual shapes, jumps, or unexpected flares.

If you're burning the flame on a wood wick, make a note of any loud or insistent crackles or hissing. Be descriptive enough that, when it comes time to interpret the signs, you have enough information to go on.

Again, while you won't interpret the signs or complete your final reading until after the ritual is over, you should still record any remarkable or interesting events that happen during it, including anything notable that happens outside the scope of the defined ritual.

An example of this may be a particularly bright sunbeam that comes through a window to shine directly on your candle.

Back in chapter one, I mentioned that there are two general types of auspicia, or signs. The first are called auspicia impetrativa. These are, to put it simply, the signs that you have asked Vesta to reveal within the templum. They are part of the formal candle divination ritual.

The second type of signs is called auspicia oblativa. These are more spontaneous signs, unsolicited and unexpected, which the divinity may send during the ritual but that may be seen, heard, or felt, outside the templum or even outside the finis.

I remember a particular reading at a friend's house, a reading we were performing in her sunroom. We had no sooner begun the spectio stage when a chickadee landed on a branch just outside the window and began singing in the loudest, most orchestral fashion you've ever heard spring forth from such a tiny body.

The little guy's persistence and happy song continued throughout the entire spectio stage. Afterward, we researched the symbolism of the chickadee and were not surprised to find this spritely little creature symbolizes cheerfulness and positivity.

And that unexpected sign—that auspicia oblativa—was more meaningful to my friend than anything else in the candle divination. She had wanted to do a reading because she had recently finalized her divorce, thus ending a twenty-year marriage. Her question to Vesta was, "Will I meet another man?"

While the auspicia impetrativa, or solicited signs, from the burn were subtle (although in her favor), it was this unsolicited and unexpected sign from Vesta—all those persistently happy chirps and that adorable feather puffing—that really spoke to her.

This sign told her to be happy. To be carefree. To stop worrying and obsessing over whether she would meet another man.

Whether she did or didn't, she needed to be more joyful and less serious. She needed to be comfortable with, and love, herself.

And as the chickadee finished his serenade and flew off to join his companions, she decided to do the same. She ended up booking a trip to France with some female friends and they flew off together. To have *fun*. To sing on a few branches in style.

So stay on alert for auspicia oblativa!

Now back to our ritual. At the end of the spectio stage, when you've reached the stipulated time limit of the burn, you should tell Vesta that you are ending the ritual. You can do this by thanking her for her presence and for the signs she has sent.

You should say aloud:

"Divine Vesta, thank you."
In Latin, this is *Gratias tibi ago, divina Vesta.*

A candle snuffer should be used to gently extinguish the flame. As the snuffer is removed from the wick, you should carefully observe the vapor and record in which direction in moves, whether you see any shapes within it, and so on.

3. *Coniectura.* The coniectura stage is the third and final stage in a formal candle divination ritual. This is when the actual "reading" happens.

This is when you will use your divination grid as a guide or template—from above, using the wick to center the grid—to read and record where on the candle's templum certain signs, in the form of wax changes, appear.

The coniectura stage is also when you will complete the reading by interpreting the signs in a way that means something to you in a practical, usable sense (e.g. the signs are favorable—I should take that trip!) and by creating a final written *summarium*, or report, of your reading.

It is this entire stage—coniectura—that is the focus of the next chapter. Why? Because recording, reading, and interpreting the signs requires a blend of formal skill and informal subjectivity. It's a big enough subject that it warrants its own chapter.

Vitia (singular: vitium)

Before we move on to the specifics of reading and interpreting the signs in that third coniectura stage, there is one last thing I need to mention here, and that's the concept of *vitia*.

Let's say you've set up your finis, marked off your templum, and you're just about to strike a match to light the wick when you accidentally drop the match or knock the box of matches onto the floor. Or perhaps all is going smoothly, but you forget to thank Vesta and thus properly end the ritual before you extinguish the flame.

Well, I hate to be the bearer of bad news, but this is called a *vitium*. It's a mistake. Roman priests and priestesses took any kind of vitium very seriously, so seriously, in fact, that the entire ritual would be abandoned and would be performed on another day.

And you should do the same. Whether the mistake is something seemingly innocuous, like forgetting your journal in another room, or whether it's more clearly problematic, like forgetting to sprinkle salt in the finis, any vitium requires you to end the ritual. Moreover, you should wait at least a day before attempting the ritual again.

CHAPTER FIVE

Candle Divination:
Reading & Interpreting the Signs

The third and final stage of candle divination is called coniectura. This is the interpretation stage, from which comes our word conjecture. It is a reasoned way of reaching a conclusion, sometimes a subjective one: it is an inference or even a thought-out guess, one we make based on the signs we have been given as well as on our own intuition. That's a powerful combination of forces.

Of course, mastering any practice, including candle divination and reading and interpreting signs, also means mastering the terminology used in that practice. I'll go through some essential terminology here: some of this is terminology borrowed from ancient augury and divination and adapted for candle divination.

As you go through this material (some of it should already be familiar to you), you will also find that I've provided you with some nice examples, as well as an inventory of signs and symbols that you can consult during your readings and interpretations. I think you'll find this to be very useful reference material.

Sinistra vs. Dextera

In Latin, *sinistra* means the left, while *dextera* means the right. When the auspices were being taken, the region of the sky to the augur's left was thus sinistra. (Do **not** be thrown by the "sinister" sound of sinistra/left. Sinistra *does not* mean bad or sinister here—it just means left.) The region of the sky to his right was dextera.

If the augur faced eastward, the north portion of the sky— where the gods resided—was to his left. This meant that signs on his left were favorable or more significant. If the augur faced southward, the east portion of the sky—where the sun rises—was to his left. This also meant that signs on his left were favorable or more significant.

In the same way, signs that appear in the two left quadrants of the templum when performing a candle divination should be interpreted as favorable or at least more significant.

Yet it's important to remember that signs which appear on the left or right need not always be interpreted in a strictly good (left) vs. bad (right) sense, or in a yes (left) vs. no (right) way.

They may be interpreted that way if the question and circumstances allow it, but there may be times when a left or right sign merely indicates that a certain situation or eventuality is in some way more significant (left) or less significant (dextera).

For example, if you've asked the specific question "Should I accept this job offer?" and the signs appear on the left, you may interpret that as a favorable / yes sign.

But what if you haven't asked a specific question? What if you're performing the divination ritual just to get a general reading or to look for signs that may reflect what is happening in your life in a more general sense?

In that case, signs that appear on the left may suggest that something favorable or significant is happening in your life: perhaps it has already happened, perhaps it is happening now, or perhaps it is about to happen.

To glean more from this kind of general reading, you can study the wax in more detail to look for further wax formations or movements that may provide more information. The list of signs, symbols, letters, and numbers that I'll present later in this chapter will help you refine your reading in this way.

Similarly, in the next heading (antica vs. postica), you'll learn to refine your reading by establishing whether the signs are relevant to your past, present, or future. This will apply whether you asked a specific question or are doing a general reading.

Antica vs. Postica

In Latin, *antica* means in front while *postica* means behind. When the auspices were being taken, and regardless of whether the augur was facing south or east, the region of the sky before him was called antica and the region behind him was called postica.

In my Vesta-based method of candle divination, which uses east as the primary orientation, the two antica quadrants represent a forward momentum, or the future. The two postica quadrants represent a backward momentum, or the past. This holds true whether you are doing a primary or secondary burn.

Reading the Quadrants of the Templum

The preceding illustration shows how to label the quadrants of the templum. These quadrants are: antica-sinistra (top left); postica-sinistra (bottom left); antica-dextera (top right), and; postica-dextera (bottom right).

Labeling the quadrants in this way is of immeasurable help when it comes to interpreting what signs in each quadrant may mean. As importantly, it can help you do this in a fairly precise way.

For example, let's imagine a candle divination in which, during the invocatio stage, the subject of the ritual asks, "Will my boyfriend ask me to marry him?"

After the spectio stage is over, she extinguishes the candle to read and interpret the signs. Using her divination grid as her guide, she studies the wax on her candle and finds a wax spike on the capital in the antica-sinistra quadrant of the templum.

She also finds a number of thick waxicles running down the column in the same antica-sinistra quadrant, although these are located in the extreme antica or forward position, almost straddling the imaginary line into the antica-dextera quadrant. What could this mean?

I would interpret these signs to say, "Yes, your boyfriend will ask you to marry him, but it may not be for some time yet."

I would arrive at this interpretation because sinistra (left) signs are favorable, while antica (forward) signs indicate the future.

An oversimplified and superficial, but nonetheless helpful, way to interpret the quadrants of the templum is as follows:

Antica-sinistra: future favorable / yes / more significant

Antica-dextera: future unfavorable / no / less significant

Postica-sinistra: past favorable / yes / more significant

Postica-dextera: past unfavorable / no / less significant

For another example, let's imagine a candle divination in which, during the invocatio stage, the subject of the reading asks, "I know management made some cuts on Friday...am I going to get laid off when I go into the office on Monday morning?"

During the spectio stage, he sees the flame sway several times into the antica-sinistra quadrant. When the spectio stage is over, he extinguishes the candle to read and interpret the signs.

Using his divination grid as his guide, he studies the wax on his candle and finds a notable wax spike in the capital in the postica-dextera quadrant of the templum.

He also finds the wick is curled toward the antica-sinistra quadrant.

What could these opposing signs be saying?

I would interpret the wax spike in the postica-dextera (bottom right) quadrant as a sign that his job may have been in jeopardy in the past (perhaps on Friday); however, the curl of the wick toward the antica-sinistra (top left) quadrant and the swaying of the flame into the same quadrant during the ritual may be signs that he survived the downsizing and won't lose his job.

Yet it's essential for the subject of the candle reading herself or himself—that's you!—to complete the final interpretation.

You are obviously the best person to put the reading as a whole into the context of your life, using what you know, and your intuition, to make sense of it all. I mention this only because candle readings are often done in a group with friends.

While you can help each other ponder the signs—that's half the fun!—you are the authority in your own life.

In the reading I just referenced, for example, the subject of the reading may interpret things very differently than I would.

It may be that he has been privately thinking about starting his own company for some time now. Perhaps his intuition has for months been telling him that he is going to lose his job as the company downsizes, and so he had better prepare for that.

He may thus interpret this reading in a way that confirms what his little voice has been telling him—yes, you're going to get laid off on Monday morning!—but he may also find the reading encouraging, as the flame points him toward a brighter future—one where he is his own boss.

Sinistra

The word sinistra doesn't just refer to the left direction—it is also the word used to describe favorable signs. Favorable signs are therefore *sinistra* signs. This is where we get the expression "the lucky left."

It's important to remember, though, that sinistra signs don't just mean "yes" or "good." As I've already said, they can also indicate significance or importance in a more general or subjective sense. It all depends on the question and the reading as a whole.

Since I know you're wondering why the word sinistra—which smacks of the word sinister—has a dark tone (outside of divination, at least), it's because the ancient Romans often associated the right-hand side of things, including the body, with dominance and more positivity.

For example, Caesar Augustus reportedly felt it was good luck to put his right sandal on first, before his left. Such contradictions and complexities were the norm in ancient Rome.

When it came to augury, though, favorable signs appeared on the left and were thus called sinistra. So we'll follow suit.

Auspicia Impetrativa

These are signs that you have clearly and deliberately asked for during the invocatio stage, and will thus observe within the boundaries of the templum. These include the types of wax changes you might expect to see on the various parts of your candle as Vesta's flame melts it—so waxicles, spikes, slopes, cracks, etc.

In the previous chapter, I described an invocatio stage that is fairly open. I explained that you can either ask a specific question of Vesta, or if you are doing a general reading, you can simply inform Vesta that you are awaiting the signs.

Nonetheless, you are free to be more particular and ask for certain or more precise signs during the invocatio stage.

For example, if you are burning a molded candle that has a unique feature on the column—perhaps a carved flower—you might say, "Vesta, I ask that you touch this flower on the candle's column if the signs are favorable."

If the carved flower on the candle's column then shows any wax changes, such as waxicles forming over it, those signs are also auspicia impetrativa—you have clearly and deliberately asked for them. (You would also interpret them as sinistra, as they are favorable based on the terms you set out.)

Auspicia Oblativa

These are signs that you did not ask for during the invocatio stage. They are unsolicited signs that may show either the goddess's approval or disapproval—so they may be favorable or unfavorable, depending on context and your interpretation. Auspicia oblativa may appear outside the templum and even outside the finis.

You may recall my anecdote about the chickadee that would not stop singing during my friend's candle divination ritual. That was an auspicious sign, one sent by Vesta of her own accord.

Auspicia oblativa may be loud and unmistakable. Perhaps you see and hear a bolt of lightning outside your window, to your left, during the invocatio or spectio stage. I would take that as a favorable sign!

At the same time, auspicia oblativa may be quiet and subtle. Perhaps you hear a brief and barely audible pop during the spectio stage and look up, to your right, to find the bulb in a ceiling light has burned out. I would take this as an unfavorable sign.

This second scenario, in particular, shows how important it is to establish and maintain that quality of silentium during a candle divination. You don't want to miss anything. Let the signs and your intuition work together to create an ideal environment for divination.

Auspicia oblativa usually take precedence over other signs. For example, if you saw large waxicles on the right but an auspicia oblativa happened on the left—perhaps that bolt of lightning I just mentioned—the signs should be interpreted as favorable.

This is because the ancient Romans placed paramount importance on strange or spontaneous signs. Whether it was the birth of a two-headed foal or the appearance of a comet, they interpreted these notable events as strong and purposeful signs from the gods.

Ostenta (singular: ostentum)

Ostenta are signs that have a very notable or novel quality to them. They are a form of auspicia impetrativa and happen within the boundaries of the templum; however, they may not appear in all burns. Ostenta are clearly seen and experienced by the subject of the reading—thus our word ostensible. They often provoke an emotional response, as if they are trying to "show" you something.

Ostenta may be good or bad, and need to be interpreted in the coniectura stage. That being said, ostenta as seen in candle divination are usually favorable and carry great weight. Because their appearance often provokes a sense of surprise, awe, or wonder, they have qualities of *miracula* (singular *miraculum*), a type of sign that similarly provokes a sense of wonder and provides the basis of our word miracle.

For example, think back to the example where you asked Vesta to touch the carved flower on a candle's column if the signs were favorable. If during the burn the wax on the capital suddenly shifted to send an abundant river of wax flowing over the carved flower, this would be an *ostentum.*

In this case, the sign is somewhat expected in the sense that you asked for it and it happens within the templum: nonetheless, its appearance is surprising (or miraculous!) and novel enough that it is going to have a strong, positive emotional impact on you.

Another example: in the preface, I shared a story about a fracture which appeared in the wax of a tealight I was burning. A river of wax spilled out to form what I immediately interpreted as the letter V, for Vesta. I would also classify this as an ostentum.

Even though the wax flowed to the right, I nonetheless felt the V shape was novel and auspicious enough to interpret this ostentum as a favorable sign, particularly as the V-shaped sign was a very personal and even emotional one for me.

Prodigia (singular: prodigium)

Prodigia are signs that are spontaneous and not asked for, and thus a form of auspicia oblativa. Prodigia are clearly seen and experienced by the subject of the reading, but unlike ostenta, they can happen outside the templum and finis, and are generally interpreted to be unfavorable in some way (e.g. a lightbulb that burns out, on your right, during the ritual.)

Prodigia may be warnings or "red flags," signs that are meant to draw your attention to something you're doing wrong, especially something that may be harmful or not in your best interests.

Omens

Omens are signs that can be either good or bad. A person can therefore see or receive a "good omen" or a "bad omen." Signs such as lightning, the sudden appearance of a meaningful bird, or the two-headed foal and comet I mentioned earlier—these can be called omens. So can notable signs in the flame, wax or vapor. The term omen is therefore a versatile one which can be used in various ways during a candle reading and which can overlap with other terms.

Omens can also be seen in life in a larger sense, outside of a candle divination. For example: "My favorite song came on the radio as soon as I began my road trip…that's a good omen!"

Waxicles

I have found that waxicles tend to form and are often most dramatic on taper candles. Regardless of the candle type you choose, however, you will likely see more waxicles with paraffin or paraffin-blend wax, although they do appear with other candle waxes as well.

Waxicles should be interpreted as favorable or unfavorable signs depending upon which quadrant or quadrants they appear in. The more of them you see, the more signs you are seeing.

If the waxicle formations you are seeing tend to be more or less evenly distributed along the candle's column, you should take a closer look at them to see whether you can notice differences in the nature of their droplet trails or paths. Waxicles which extend to the base of the candle (perhaps even pooling around the base) are more significant than those which do not.

Droplets that form a trail or trails in a straight line, or straight-ish, often indicate success or prosperity, as the finest columns in the ancient Roman world were fluted—they had scalloped lines running down their length, and were considered very ornate. If you're seeing these elements on the left, this suggests favorable or significant signs.

In contrast, a waxicle which seems to have stalled along its path or accumulated into larger formations may be interpreted to mean that an obstacle is in your path. Whether that obstacle is favorable or unfavorable, significant or insignificant, depends on what quadrant(s) you are seeing it in.

Think about it: not all obstacles are bad, are they? Some obstacles, as infuriating and discouraging as they can be, nonetheless force us to do better or try harder. That in turn results in a better outcome for us.

Other obstacles may be protective and are actually working to prevent something undesirable happening to us.

My point is, never look at a sign and say, "That's terrible!" Instead, approach your readings from all angles and put it in context. Try to find something useful and positive in all readings.

Not all readings will say, "Wonderful! Your future will be perfect!" You know that isn't how life works. Life is rarely perfect. So when you get a sign that reflects this, don't panic.

Instead, study your candle and search your intuition for messages that will help you face whatever challenges life throws at you with strength, perspective, and tenacity.

Wax Pools & Rivers

Wax that drips down the candle's column to congeal at or around the base should be read from above, with the wick in the center of the divination grid.

You can then record how much of the wax pool or river is in each quadrant. You should also examine any wax pools or rivers to see in which direction the flow is heading, and whether they form any discernable shapes.

You can also look for areas of swirls within the congealed wax pool: swirls in a counter-clockwise (left) direction generally indicate favorable or significant signs, while swirls in a clockwise (right) direction generally indicate unfavorable or insignificant signs.

Spikes to Slopes: Other Wax Formations

Depending on the candle and wax type, you may see all kind of wax activity and wax formations on your candle—spikes, sheets, slopes, folds, cracks, fractures, and so on.

All else being equal, more wax activity and/or more active wax formations equal more signs. The meaning of those signs and whether they are favorable or unfavorable depends on where they appear in the templum and in relation to one another.

For example, spikes that are actively pushed upward as the candle burns down may be signs of future success if seen in the antica-sinistra (future favorable) quadrant.

If seen in the antica-dextera (future unfavorable) quadrant, however, spikes may signify that some large or painful obstacles are in one's future.

A capital that melts and slopes to the left is a favorable sign, since Vesta's flame has been more active and burned hotter in that area, thus causing the wax to melt more and slope.

Remember that the strongest signs usually appear in those areas of the candle where Vesta's flame has burned the hottest, or where it has been the most active, thus resulting in various spikes, slopes, or other wax formations.

Once you read and record all wax activity and wax formations that appear within the templum you can interpret them in relation to one other.

And that relativity is key. There will be times when more wax activity will be less important than more modest wax activity. Remember my friend's molded "60" birthday cake candle? The one where the 6 stayed intact but the 0 melted? That was such a case.

Another example: a very large spike of wax on the capital in the favorable antica-sinistra (top left) quadrant may at first glance appear to be the predominant sign; however, the presence of a smaller but novel heart-shaped formation in the unfavorable antica-dextera (top right) quadrant may in fact be more meaningful.

Despite the showy spike in the future-favorable quadrant, the subject of the reading may (and should!) put more weight on the much more subtle heart sign in the unfavorable-future quadrant, since this is an ostentum. It's trying to show him something.

He may interpret the signs as saying he needs to strengthen his relationship so that he and his partner can face any future challenges together, before any problems can spiral out of control. If they can do this, they will be rewarded with an even stronger and happier relationship in the future.

The Flame & Vapor

It may seem incongruous that although Vesta resides in the flame and not the wax, it is largely the wax that we read for signs. Then again, it is very likely that the Vestals diligently studied the burnt wood in the sacred hearth.

The Vestals likely studied the ash as well: we know they kept the ash from the sacred fire in a special depository under the temple (called the *favissa*) and had a special ritual to dispose of it in the Tiber River.

The way we study the wax touched by Vesta's eternal flame is therefore no different than the way the ancients studied the wood and ash touched by her flame.

Yet it is essential to observe, record, and interpret the behavior of the flame on the wick as well. Make sure you keep your candle wick(s) trimmed to the manufacturer's recommendations so that it is burning and supporting the flame as it should.

Watch for movements in the flame and the direction of those movements. A flame that moves or sways to the left is just as auspicious, perhaps even more so, than a waxicle, spike, or wax pool on the left.

Observe the strength and posture of the flame. A strong, straight, stable flame on a cotton wick is a sign of clarity, constancy, and peace. If you see it, it is likely a good sign.

Watch for flares, flickers, and jumping flames too, especially on wood wicks. A dancing flame may be a sign that Vesta is trying to motivate or energize you...to give you a kick in your complacency! It may also be a sign of excitement that something good is on the horizon.

Study the flame for shapes. Although it doesn't happen too often, you may occasionally see a recognizable form within a swaying or jumping flame.

If you are using a wood wick, listen to the crackles, snaps, sizzles, and hisses. As a general rule, the louder the flame the better, as this is the voice of Vesta speaking. Look carefully at the wick and note if you see any red embers on it—these are good signs.

When it is time to extinguish your flame with the snuffer, watch for Vesta's breath in the form of vapor as it swirls up and away. Note what direction it moves in, and look carefully for any discernable shapes. They may be fleeting, but they are meaningful.

Finally, look for any bits of burnt wick that have broken off to land in the wax of the capital, and note their location within the templum. These wick bits should be considered favorable omens— they are signs that Vesta is on your side!

Symbols & Shapes

While it is always satisfying to see strong signs in the wax—from waxicles to spikes and everything in between—it is always a special and novel experience to see a wax formation that clearly and unmistakably takes the shape of a recognizable symbol. A recognizable symbol or shape is usually classified as an ostentum.

Indeed, the ancient Romans who honored Vesta loved their symbols almost as much as their gods and goddesses. In fact, they combined these two great loves by giving each god and goddess his or her own special animal or other element as a symbol.

For example, Minerva, the goddess of wisdom, was symbolized by an owl, which remains a symbol of wisdom today.

Seeing an owl shape in your wax reading is therefore a very exciting and fulfilling thing. It's also a fairly strong message, since it indicates that wisdom—either an abundance of it or a lack of it—is somehow factoring into your life. Depending on what quadrant(s) this sign appears in, it may be suggesting that your wisdom is about to pay off, or it may be encouraging you to wise up!

In my experience, some of the best symbols and shapes appear when I am performing a candle wax dripping in water. You'll learn about this in the next chapter.

Yet I've seen some beauties when doing a divination with pillars, tapers, and molded candles as well. I've even seen recognizable symbols and shapes appear on the inside rim of the glass after a container candle divination.

Of course, there are many formations you may see come and go during your burn, or congeal to become permanent. You will interpret many of these in your own way, depending upon what is on your mind or what is going on in your life.

Don't be afraid to use your imagination and guess a little! Even Cicero admits the "best diviner" is often the best guesser!

Nonetheless, I would like to present you with an inventory of symbols from the ancient world, ones that I believe are particularly valuable and relevant to the type of candle divination we are doing here.

Actively look for these symbols in your reading. If you see them, consider yourself very blessed! Always strive to interpret them in the larger context of your life to determine their relevance.

Thunderbolt This suggests power or supremacy, as it is the symbol of Jupiter, father of all the gods.

Eagle Another symbol of Jupiter, and the emblem of the Roman army, this similarly suggests power or supremacy, as well as victory.

Oak leaves or a tree This suggests authority, since the ancient kings wore crowns of oak; the oak tree was sacred to them. A tree can also symbolize growth or some kind of expansion in your personal or professional life.

Peacock The peacock is the symbol of Juno, goddess of women, marriage, and childbirth. Look for shapes that resemble the parts of a peacock, whether the bird's long neck or distinctive feathers. Seeing these may be relevant to matters of marriage and/or motherhood.

Owl The owl is a symbol of wisdom, and is associated with the goddess of wisdom, Minerva.

Donkey ears The donkey is associated with Vesta: seeing shapes that look like donkey ears or a tail may therefore be indicative of issues surrounding the home. Because Vesta's eternal fire is also a symbol of the eternal soul, seeing donkey ears may be indicative of more introspective, philosophical, or spiritual matters. Finally, seeing a donkey (or parts of a donkey) in the wax may allude to stubbornness—are you being too stubborn or not stubborn enough?

Wolf This is a powerful symbol, as it was the symbol of the god of war, Mars. Seeing a wolf's nose, ears, or even tail, may suggest aggression of some kind—perhaps it is directed toward you, or perhaps it is a sign that you need to assert yourself more.

Shield or sword Instruments of war or battle are associated with the god of war, Mars. As is the case when seeing a wolf, these signs may be warning signs or they may be encouraging you to be wary or "on guard" and act in your own best interests.

Wheat, grain or seeds These are the symbols of Ceres, goddess of the grain crops and also of fertility. Seeing these symbols can be auspicious if you are embarking on a new financial venture or trying to conceive.

Sickle The sickle is another symbol of Ceres, a complicated goddess associated with the underworld. Seeing a sickle may indicate you need to spend more time pondering deeper issues in your life.

Bow and arrow While instruments of war are usually associated with Mars, the bow and arrow is also the symbol of Diana, goddess of the hunt and of animals. If you have pets, this symbol may relate to them in some way.

Crescent moon Another symbol of Diana, goddess of the hunt, seeing a crescent moon could indicate you need to search or "hunt" for something a little harder before you will find it. It may also indicate you need to put more effort into something, whether a personal or professional goal, before you will achieve it.

Wings The Roman god Mercury is often depicted with winged sandals. The god of travelers, signs associated with him may indicate a trip of some kind. Mercury is also the god of commerce, so seeing wings may allude to financial matters.

Trident   The trident is the symbol of Neptune, god of the sea. Seeing his symbol may suggest something to do with water or the sea, whether it's encouraging you to spend some relaxing time at the beach (or in the bath!) or take an overseas trip. Because water is the element necessary to support life, this symbol may also be a sign that you should take better care of yourself—drink more water!

Fish or sea life   These are also associated with Neptune.

Horse   Another symbol of Neptune, the god associated with horse racing in Rome. Because Neptune had an unpredictable and aggressive nature, seeing a horse in your candle wax or vapor may be a sign that you need to move away—quickly!—from this kind of behavior, whether you're seeing it in yourself or someone else. It could also mean the opposite—that you need to "charge toward" or "race toward" something more assertively if you want to "win" it.

Hammer or ax   These symbols represent Vulcan, the god of fire and the blacksmith of the gods; Vulcan created the gods' various weapons. Vulcan also has the unenviable distinction of being the "ugly" god. Seeing a hammer or ax shape can mean a couple things. It may mean that you need to address any ugliness in your life, whatever that means to you. It may also mean that you need to focus on creating or building something in your life or career.

Lyre A lyre is a stringed U-shaped instrument that is a very common symbol of Apollo. Apollo is a very important and multifaceted god: he is variously the god of music, art, healing, and the sun. Seeing a symbol indicative of Apollo could thus be a sign of many things in your life, from creativity to well-being.

Sun or rays of light As the sun god, rays of light radiated out of Apollo's head as each morning he rode his golden horse-drawn chariot across the sky, bringing the sun up with it. Seeing wax formations that resemble the sun, or rays of light, can thus indicate a new beginning or a fresh start of some kind.

Rose One of the most common symbols of Venus, goddess of love, seeing a rose usually refers to matters surrounding romantic relationships. It can also refer to fertility.

Seashell A symbol of Venus, shells represent her birth from the sea.

Snake A snake can be a sign that signifies protectiveness: snakes were often seen as guardians of the temples and other sacred sites. A snake sign may suggest that you need to protect or care for yourself in some way. A snake is also a sign of growth, renewal or transformation—just think of a snake shedding its old skin for a shiny new one. A snake symbol may be a sign that you are changing somehow, or that you should change in some way to better yourself.

Column Seeing a column shape in your candle wax, flame, or vapor, indicates strength and support. It may be a sign that you need to find the strength to do something, or that you need to support yourself or someone else. It may also be a reminder that you are stronger than you think!

Mask The mask was a common symbol of the arts in the ancient world, just as it is today. Yet a mask can also refer to "performance" in a more philosophical sense—are you pretending to be someone you're not, or playing a role you don't want to play? Seeing a mask shape during your divination may be a sign to get out there, on stage, and be brave! It may also be a sign that it's time to take off the mask and be your true self.

Knot The knot was a symbol of Hercules: when a couple married in ancient Rome, the bride belted her dress with the "knot of Hercules," a knot that only her husband could untie. If you see a knot in your divination ritual, it may therefore be a symbol of true, strong, love—whether the one you have or the one you're destined to have. It could also be a sign that you need to love yourself and find strength in that.

Tunneling

You've seen a candle that tunnels before—it's when only the wax around the wick, in the center of the candle, melts, so that you have coring down the middle of the candle as it burns.

Major tunneling is often symptomatic of a low quality candle, especially one with an improperly sized wick. But it can also happen by incorrectly burning a candle and especially by not burning it long enough on its initial burn.

Because you won't be reusing your candle for another divination ritual, this may not be a huge concern for you. Yet you should still read the candle manufacturer's first-burn recommendations before lighting your ritual candle so that you can ensure your divination goes as smoothly as possible.

If you've done everything properly but tunneling still occurs, it may be a sign that you're engaging in some kind of self-destructive or even overly self-focused behavior, or that you're being too impulsive or obsessive in some area of your life, especially if the tunneling seems to slope to the right.

Tunneling that slopes to the left may suggest the opposite: you need to be more headstrong! You will need to interpret this sign with respect to what quadrant(s) it leans into and what other signs you see, as well as in the context of what is happening in your life.

Letters

According to the ancient biographer Suetonius, the emperor Augustus foretold his own death when he saw an eagle land on the letter A of an inscription on a temple. Indeed, there is something symbolic about letters, particularly the first letter of our own name.

If you see the first letter of your name in your candle wax, flame, or vapor, do your best to interpret it alongside the other signs you see. That's because seeing the first letter of your name can be a sign of amplification or emphasis.

For example, if your name is Sophia and you see the letter S near the shape of a hammer in the antica-sinistra (top left) quadrant of the templum, it could be a sign that you need to forge a new life (or career, or home, or relationship, or lifestyle, etc.) for yourself, if you want your future to be a happy one.

In this scenario, the S is for emphasis—Vesta's flame is telling you, Sophia, in no uncertain terms, that she is talking to you! So do it. Make a change.

Seeing a letter during a divination can also be a catalyst of sorts: it encourages you to dig a little deeper, to think about what the letter stands for or represents.

If you see an H, for example, you may not immediately know what it signifies. Yet once you give it some thought, once you let your intuition work it out, the meaning will come to the forefront.

You may realize the H is a sign that you need to focus on getting *h*ealthier. Or it may be encouraging you to spoil yourself and try something new, maybe a new *h*airstyle. Not all signs need to be serious!

A letter may also represent another person's name, an event, or a circumstance that is in some way impacting your life.

A person who sees the letter D in the postica-dextera (bottom left) quadrant may not immediately know what that means. Yet after tapping into their intuition, they may come to realize that they have never quite gotten over their *d*ivorce, and that they're essentially stuck in the past.

This may therefore signify the need to put the past behind them and move on with life.

Letters can also represent emotions, actions, and characteristics. If you see a P, it may be that you need to be more *p*atient in life. You get the idea.

So if you're lucky enough to see a letter during your divination, go through the alphabet—and your life—and figure out what it means. That is what "divining" your life is about!

Numbers

Numbers, like all symbols, are attributed different meanings in different cultures, religions, and philosophies.

In Western culture, we often regard the number 7 as lucky, but the number 13 as unlucky, sometimes going so far as to omit floor 13 from buildings or skip over room 13 in hotels.

And be honest: don't you drive a little more cautiously on Friday the 13th? Don't you remind your kids or friends to be a little extra careful?

Numbers are also attributed different meanings depending on your purpose. Using numbers to determine an auspicious date for your wedding is very different than using numbers to send a spacecraft to the moon!

Numerology is a complicated system that seeks to reveal information about your life via numbers, not unlike the way astrology seeks to reveal information about your life via the stars and planets. When I speak about numbers and candle divination, I am not referring to numerology.

For our purposes here, seeing numbers in your candle wax, flame, or vapor, is very much like seeing letters (or any other recognizable shape or symbol, for that matter) in them. It is an ostentum or an omen—a catalyst sign, one that prompts you to put it into the context of your life and the reading as a whole.

The scenario that immediately comes to mind for me is of a woman who was wondering whether she and her husband should have a third child. They had two boys, but she secretly wondered whether her husband wanted a daughter. She tried to ask him about it, but he only said, "Whatever you want."

During her candle reading, the unmistakable figure of the number 3 appeared—but it appeared in the antica-dextera (top right) quadrant of the templum, indicating an unfavorable future. She interpreted this as a cautionary sign, which in turn compelled her to have a more assertive and honest conversation with her husband.

She told him the truth. She didn't want a third child. She knew she could be a good mom to two kids, but she was worried that she would be overwhelmed with three. The only reason she wanted to try again was to please him in case he secretly wanted a daughter.

Her husband could not have been more relieved to hear her say this. He told her that he didn't want a third child either. He had only said "Whatever you want" because he wanted her to be happy, in case she secretly wanted to try again. But like her, he was worried about the toll a third child would have on their family and finances.

I think this is a perfect example of how a candle reading can work in conjunction with your intuition—that little voice—to help you face and focus on your problems, and to work through the questions you have to arrive at answers that bring you happiness and peace.

Remember, though, that the ancients who honored Vesta did not use Arabic numerals like we do. They of course used Roman numerals. So look for these in the wax too!

In case you aren't familiar with Roman numerals, I'll list numbers one to ten here.

I	One
II	Two
III	Three
IV	Four
V	Five
VI	Six
VII	Seven
VIII	Eight
IX	Nine
X	Ten

A few of these numerals are very special signs, so I'll spend a few moments talking about them. The first special sign is the Roman numeral II (two). This is the soul-mate number—not a surprise when you consider how it resembles two figures standing closely together to form a columnar shape (remember the column is a sign of strength).

Seeing a II is therefore a good omen, whether it refers to a romantic soul-mate or someone or something that is very close to you, that supports you. This is someone or something that brings meaning and companionship to your life.

The second special Roman numeral is V (five). This is particularly auspicious. It is the letter V for Vesta, but it also symbolizes an open hand with spread fingers.

This can be a sign that you are about to receive something or that you are grasping for something that will soon be within your reach—another good omen.

The third Roman numeral that you should consider a special sign, and a good omen, is the numeral VII (seven). Rome was built on seven hills—the famous *septem colles* or *montes Romae*. The first, the Palatine Hill, offered a bird's eye view of the Temple of Vesta directly below in the Forum. The Romans celebrated their seven hills in a festival called the *Septimontium*.

The ancient Romans also associated the number seven with renewal, believing that life renewed itself every seven years.

Seeing the number seven during your divination ritual may therefore signify a great endeavor or feat of some kind. It may also symbolize some sort of renewal or new beginning, whether in terms of lifestyle, relationship, emotions, mindset, or finances.

Intuition & Interpretation

There are countless ways to interpret the meaning of shapes, symbols, letters, and numbers. Even a symbol as common as a heart won't have the same meaning to all people.

A person struggling with a relationship issue will probably think of love when they see a heart shape. A person struggling with a health issue, or worried about their health, may think of that when they see this symbol.

A person's culture, age, spiritual outlook, personal experience and philosophy, and so on, can also affect the meaning that he or she attributes to a symbol.

For example, the snake is a power symbol of protection and renewal in some belief systems, yet it is demonized in others. Before the 1930's in the Western world, the swastika—an ancient spiritual symbol in Eurasian culture—was a symbol of luck. Now, well, you know. My point is, there is no single definitive interpretation of any shape, symbol, letter, or number.

While I hope you will find the inventory of symbols I've presented here helpful and meaningful, in the end, you must follow your first instinct and your intuition when you see a shape in the wax, flame, or vapor.

That's one reason I encourage you to use beeswax candles when you can: their ability to enhance intuition can be very useful and revealing during a candle divination.

Even if you don't want to use beeswax for divination, you can still have a beeswax candle burning within the finis you've established.

You can even use four beeswax tealights or votive candles in lieu of stones to create the square or rectangular area of your finis. In this way, you can receive the benefits of beeswax-enhanced intuition while still being able to perform the actual divination ritual on a non-beeswax candle.

Regardless of what you choose to do, just remember that this book is called *Divining YOUR Life* for a reason! It is *your* life. You know it best. When you see a shape, symbol, letter, or number, trust yourself and your interpretation of it. The only thing I insist on is that you always try to find the good, the positive, and the encouraging, in each and every reading. It's in there somewhere.

The Summarium

After you have; a) established the parameters of your ritual and invoked Vesta; b) carefully watched for signs during the burn and the spectio stage, and; c) read and interpreted the signs in the coniectura stage, it is time to complete the divination ritual by creating a written summary of your reading. This is called the summarium.

Your summarium should be handwritten (or typewritten and then printed out) and kept in your journal, and should include the following:

• the date, time, orientation and other particulars or parameters of the ritual

• the type of candle, candle wax, and wick you used

• the specific question(s) you asked Vesta to answer

• if you were doing a general reading, were there any particular issues or matters you had in mind while you awaited the signs?

• a written description of signs, as recorded on the divination grid: this includes a description of wax formations (e.g. spikes, waxicles, slopes, shifts, cracks, fractures, pools or rivers, etc.) as well as their location in the templum

• any auspicia oblativa

• any ostenta, particularly any that provoke an emotional response

• any omens or prodigia

• the behavior of the flame during the burn (e.g. tall and steady, short and sputtering, whether it danced or leaned into certain quadrants of the templum, whether it crackled, etc.)

• a description of the flame's vapor during the burn, or after extinguishment: in which directions did it move, and did you see any shapes in the vapor?

• whether any burnt wax bits fell into the wax, and where

• the answer to your specific question, as you interpreted it from the signs (e.g. yes or no, favorable or not, important or not, an event that happened in the past vs. one that will happen in the future, etc.)

• if you did a general reading, a description of what the signs were suggesting (e.g. something significant has happened or will happen, I should think about taking a trip, I should relax more, etc.)

• your personal feelings about the reading: did it confirm what your intuition was telling you?

• the takeaway: what did you learn or come to realize during the course of the divination ritual that may help you move forward in a positive way?

• the plan: are there any areas of your life you need to work on? Are there any changes you need to make? If so, make a note of them. Be honest—your journal is good for recording and interpreting the signs, but it can also be a good place to write down your personal thoughts, feelings, and intentions

• anything else you feel is relevant

CHAPTER SIX

Bringing It All Together

Candle Divination: A Walk-Through

I'd like to bring all the information you've learned so far together now, in what is essentially a mental walk-through or overview of a candle divination. Here, I will repeat—for the purpose of reinforcement—the procedure I have already outlined. This time as you read, however, I want you to imagine yourself actually performing all of these various steps. The more you can mentally immerse yourself in it, the more you will be able to remember and make sense of the process when it's your turn to do it.

Even if you're already confident in your ability to perform a candle reading, I encourage you to at least skim this chapter, and definitely take a peek at the illustrations I've included.

To help you visualize the walk-through, you can imagine we're using a standard white high-grade paraffin wax pillar or taper candle with a cotton wick (although of course all of this can be adapted for almost all manner of wax and candle types).

Let's get started.

Gather all your supplies: your candle, compass, termini, salt shaker, wood matches, pen, divination grid, divination journal, candle snuffer, as well as your offerings and/or libations.

Close all the windows to protect the flame from drafts. Check that the wick is as straight as possible Since it's a cotton wick, you should be easily able to straighten it if necessary.

Use your compass to determine the east direction, and then position yourself and your candle so that you are facing east, the primary orientation. To ensure you are accurately positioning your candle, look at it from above and imagine it is the face of a clock: make sure the 12 o'clock position is facing antica (forward / east).

To encourage a lively reading, you may wish to perform this divination at dawn, when the sun is first rising in the east.

Establish the finis, or boundary, of your divination area by placing four termini, such as small decorative stones, in a square or rectangle around your candle. The finis should be large enough to also include your supplies.

Since in this case we are using a paraffin wax candle rather than beeswax, you may wish to use four beeswax tealights or votive candles as termini: this will help purify the finis—a very important thing when taking the auspices—while also enhancing your intuition so that you can better observe and interpret the signs.

Sprinkle a little salt in the finis to ritually purify the area, and set your earthenware bowl(s) of libations and/or offerings within it.

Next, use your lituus (which is most likely the handle of your candle snuffer) to ritually mark out the templum: this is the area or areas of the candle itself within which you will observe for and record the signs.

You can mark out this templum by imagining a grid of four squares laying on top of your candle, with the wick positioned in the center.

To begin the invocatio stage of the divination ritual by invoking Vesta, say:

"Visit this candle, Mother Vesta."
In Latin, this is *Invise hanc candelam, Mater Vesta.*

If you wish, you can very lightly carve a V into the wax on the column of your candle to dedicate it to Vesta, although this isn't strictly necessary.

Strike a wood match and hold the flame to the candle's wick, preferably from the left. Observe the flame as it catches fire on the wick and make a note of its behavior.

Once the flame is firmly established, you can ask your question of Vesta. If you have a specific question in mind, say:

"Vesta, if it be your will, send me an unmistakable sign within these boundaries that I have set."

After saying this, clearly ask your specific question. Let's say the question in this case is:

"Will I find true love this year?"

If you do not have a specific question in mind and are simply looking for a general reading and spontaneous signs, you can say:

"Vesta, if it be your will, I await the signs."

This is also the time to establish the time parameters for the divination. So you might say:

"To receive the signs, I will burn your flame on this candle for one hour."

Or a half-hour, or two hours…it is up to you. Be sure to keep a close eye on the clock and strictly adhere to this time period.

If you wish, you can say an extra prayer to Vesta (refer to the prayers I provided in chapter four, when I first outlined the three stages of candle divination).

Now begins the spectio stage of the ritual.

Read the flame by observing for signs within the templum you earlier marked out with your lituus.

Note how many times it sways into each of the four quadrants. Watch for any shapes and listen for any sounds. This is where you will practice pyromancy.

Be sure to record your observations on your divination grid by making a small mark in the appropriate quadrant—antica-sinistra, postica-sinistra, antica-dextera, or postica-dextera—each time the flame sways to the left or right, or up or down.

You should also make notes in your journal, the one you will keep and maintain for each and every candle divination ritual you perform.

Now turn your attention to the candle's wax, observing for signs—however, do not record these yet. Wax readings are not taken until the candle has been extinguished and the wax has completely cooled and congealed.

You will need to have chosen a burn time that is sufficient for the wax to melt and morph at least enough to produce some readable elements (e.g. spikes, folds or slopes in the capital, waxicles on the column, a little pooling of wax at the base, etc.). These elements may be subtle or obvious.

During the spectio stage, you should also do your best to tap into your own intuition and listen to your little voice—what is it telling you about the question you asked?

Instead of just waiting for signs in the wax, use this time for yourself. Use it to reflect upon the question or your life in a larger sense.

Candle divination takes time. The auspices, the signs, can take a while to appear. With some other divination methods, such as casting stones, or reading tea leaves or Tarot cards, the answers are shown fairly quickly.

Not so with candle reading (the exception is wax drippings in water, which can be performed and interpreted more quickly—I'll talk more about that soon).

In fact, it is the "slow burn" of candle divination that can make it such a useful and relevant experience. It gives you an opportunity to sequester yourself from the loud, stressful world and lose yourself in a beautiful, natural, and peaceful ritual, one that focuses on you. Enjoy it.

Instead of busying yourself cleaning the house while your candle burns, or passing the time surfing the Internet, do some soul-searching and let the silence heal you.

If it's a long burn, at least do something that complements the silence. Read that book you've been trying to get to. Or do something creative, whether writing or painting. Spend some time in the presence of the goddess. Stay near the flame.

I've been known to take a spa day while I'm doing a candle divination, letting my candle burn on the bathroom sink countertop (on a fire-safe candle tray) while I treat myself to the kind of indulgences I don't usually have time for—a manicure and pedicure, and a long soak in the bathtub. By the time I'm ready to read the signs, I'm relaxed and receptive to doing that with an open mind.

I also like doing candle divination outdoors on my stone patio. I'll choose a breezeless summer day and put my candle directly on a designated area of my stone patio where it can burn while I enjoy the sunshine. Who would want to rush a day like that?

This practice is especially suited for those times I wish to perform a good base reading, as the candle wax can melt and spread out naturally on my stone patio to create a large base pool of wax while I sip coffee and watch.

You'll want to think about doing this, though, as the wax can be difficult if not impossible to remove (I have special paving stones I use for this). As always, you should do your research and adapt the ritual to your unique circumstances and environment.

Returning now to our pillar / taper burn: while you are observing the flame and the wax, it's also important to stay alert for auspicia oblativa.

You'll recall that these are unexpected or spontaneous signs—such as a particularly lyrical chickadee or sudden sunbeam—that appears. Such signs may appear inside or outside the finis.

If you notice any, be sure to record them in your journal. When it comes time to interpret the signs, auspicia oblativa almost always take precedence over other signs, so you'll want to make sure they're well-described and well-documented in your journal

When the established time period for the burn is coming to an end, you should prepare to extinguish the flame. The flame should never go out on its own. If it does, it is a vitium or error.

If that happens, or if another error happens (e.g. you drop something on the floor, you forget to include an offering or libation within your finis, etc.) the divination should not be continued and should instead be performed anew on another day.

To extinguish the flame, you should first thank Vesta for her presence, thus signifying the end of the ritual.

You can say:

"Divine Vesta, thank you."
In Latin, this is *Gratias tibi ago, divina Vesta.*

Extinguish the flame using a candle snuffer. Do not blow on the flame to extinguish it, as you will corrupt the results by influencing the movement of the vapor and potentially even the wax.

As you remove the snuffer from the wick, observe the vapor from the flame's extinguishment.

Note in which direction(s) it moves, and record this on your divination grid. Look closely for any discernable shapes within the swirls of vapor. This is where you will practice capnomancy.

Now begins the coniectura stage of the ritual.

Wait a few minutes for any liquid wax or pools of wax to solidify.

To do a capital reading, look down at the top of the candle from above and visualize the four quadrants of the templum.

If you need a little guidance or a template, simply hold or place your divination grid next to your candle as a reference.

Study the burnt wick. If it leans, angles or curls toward a certain quadrant, draw or make a note of this on the divination grid.

Make a note of whether any bits of the wick have fallen off into the wax, and in what quadrant(s) you see them.

Now you will begin to practice true carromancy. Starting at the capital and working your way down the column to the base, "read" the candle for any spikes, slopes, waxicles, other wax formations, and/or wax pools.

Remember: as a general rule, more wax activity and active wax formations equal more signs. Yet you must interpret the significance and meaning of these within the context of the reading as a whole, tapping into your intuition to do so. Even a small ostentum (a tiny heart shape) can be more significant than a large amount of wax activity or a large active wax formation (a large spike).

Record your findings on your divination grid. In each quadrant, note how much wax is present (relative to the wax in other quadrants) and either draw or document its features. You can document in greater detail by further describing what you are seeing in your journal.

In this way, your divination grid (or grids if you use more than one) and your journal should contain complementary information that fully describes your readings.

This information should be detailed enough that you can refer back to it during subsequent divination rituals, thus tracking the history of your readings.

If you see any shapes or symbols, or notice any interesting trajectories or features of waxicles or wax trails, you should do your best to draw these on your divination grid and/or in your journal, and indicate in which quadrant(s) you saw them.

Finally, let's say that you've left your pillar or taper candle to burn long enough that a significant pool of wax has collected and congealed around the base of the candle, even extending beyond the area of the templum. Or perhaps a crack has occurred, sending a long river of wax down the column and outward from the base.

In this case, only read and record what you see within the templum. And as always, use the wick to establish the center of the divination grid, even if the position of the candle has shifted during the burn. Record any distinctive shapes, swirls, or mounds, as well as the direction or directions of flow in any wax pools or rivers.

Because the flame is a living thing, it will burn differently during each ritual with a spirit of its own—the ancient spirit of Vesta. That's why I find this form of divination so fascinating. You never know what it is going to show you.

Nonetheless, don't be tempted to look at a single sign and say "my reading is good / bad." Readings must be holistic and you must carefully read and record all of the signs so that you can interpret them in context.

Yet in practice, you will find that the process of reading and interpreting the signs happens at the same time.

Reading the signs is like reading a story. As you see and record each sign, as you see and record each word, you are simultaneously interpreting what you are reading in a way that has meaning to you. The more signs you read, the more words you read, the longer and more meaningful the story becomes.

And since you are the author of your final reading, your final step, and the final part of the coniectura stage, is to prepare a written summarium of your reading.

Before you sit down to write your summarium, feel free to stretch your legs for a few minutes or make yourself a good cup of coffee or tea. Or pour yourself a glass of wine. Get comfortable.

Now, spend some time documenting the details of your candle divination, including things like the date and time, the orientation, candle and wax type, and so on.

Include the specific question you asked, or whether you were just doing a general reading.

Write about the signs you saw and the way(s) you interpret them. Tap into your intuition to do this. When it comes to candle divination, your intuition is just as valuable as your divination grid!

Always interpret the signs in a way that helps you move forward in life—in a way that helps you heal a wound, or find peace, or feel inspired. Vesta's flame, a candle…these are beautiful things and you should get something beautiful out of the experience.

At the same time, don't blithely ignore the signs, or your intuition, when it encourages you to make a real-world change for the better, even if it's a tough one.

When you have completed your summarium, and the ritual is thus completely over, you can proceed in a couple of ways.

You can stop at this point, without moving on to perform a second burn in the secondary south-facing orientation.

Because candle divination can be a time-consuming process (especially if you're using a larger pillar or beeswax candle), this is perfectly acceptable. If you decide to stop here, great—you're finished! If, however, you wish to proceed to a reading in the secondary south-facing orientation, you can do so. Just remember that you will need a completely new candle.

Another option after completing the primary orientation burn of a time-consuming pillar or beeswax candle is to take something of a short-cut and perform a wax drippings in water reading.

This is a comparatively quick and straightforward candle divination method, yet it nonetheless provides a wealth of relevant, rewarding signs that you can compare and contrast with those observed during your previous reading. So keep this option in mind.

The chapter on candle wax drippings in water follows this one. It offers an entirely different way to perform candle wax divination, one that I find delivers particularly rewarding and dramatic readings. It's also a really fun process.

Illustrations:
Sample Candle Wax Readings

To help you better visualize the process of reading a candle and the divination grid, I am going to provide you with four illustrations that depict very simple sample candle wax readings.

Of course, your interpretations and summarium will be much more detailed. The images that follow are only meant to reinforce what you've learned in a general way.

You'll notice that I've used the same candle for all four illustrations—it is a white paraffin wax taper candle—although I've placed it in four different positions so as to make the wax formations appear in different quadrants.

We'll assume these candle wax readings were of a general nature, meaning that the subject of the reading did not ask a specific yes / no type of question, but was rather looking for a general reading of what might be going on in their life.

Again, my hope is to keep things extremely simple at this point so you can grasp the meaning of what it might mean to see wax formations in each quadrant.

Once you have a good grasp of what it means, or could mean, to see wax formations in the various quadrants, you'll be able read any candle regardless of how many or how few formations appear, or how plain or spectacular they are.

The basic principles of candle reading will not change.

Finally, always remember that candle reading is an art. Use your intuition, imagination, and your intelligence to arrive at a final reading that means something to you within the larger context of your life. That, and have fun with it!

Here, there are significant wax pools in the sinistra quadrants, although mostly postica (past). There is a notable wax pool and some waxicles in the antica-dextera quadrant, suggesting a future challenge. Drawing upon the good things in their past will help this person overcome the minor unfavorable event or circumstance they are about to face.

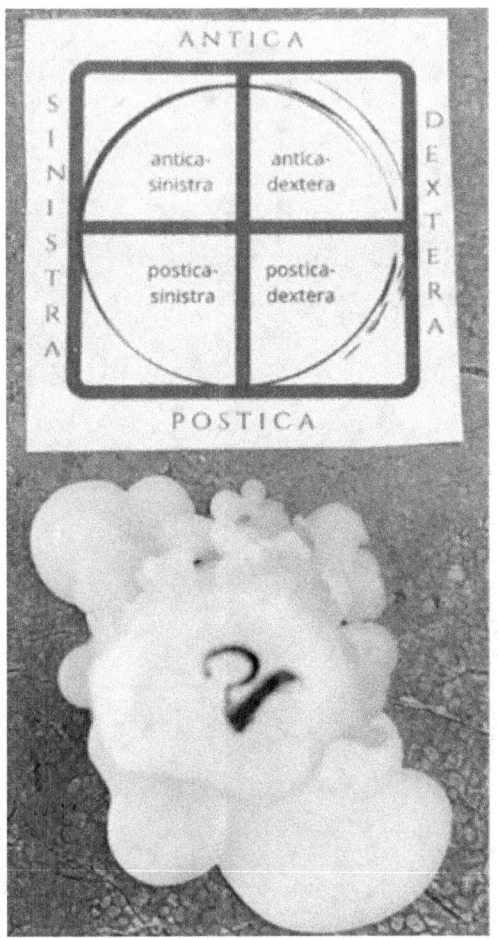

The large pool of wax in the postica-dextera quadrant
may suggest either a bad past experience or someone
who is "stuck in the past". However, the pooling of wax in
the antica-sinistra quadrant is promising this person that
if they can heal and move forward, their future will be
better and happier.

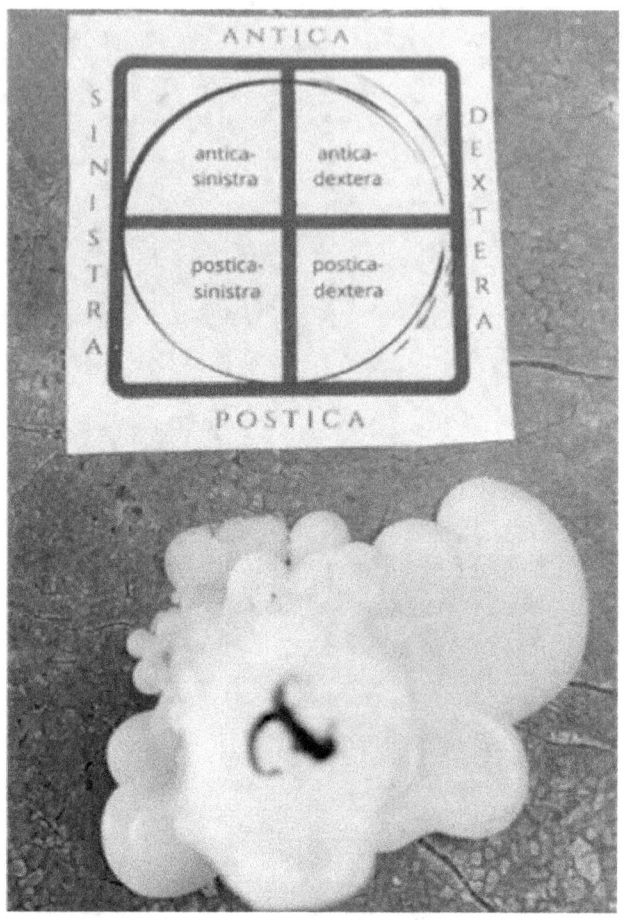

The pooling of wax in the postica quadrants indicates good and bad in this person's past; however, the flow of wax to the antica-dextera suggests some challenges lie ahead. With scenarios like this, it's important to put all readings into context - for example, if the flame swayed into the antica-sinistra quadrant during the burn, Vesta may be encouraging this individual to fight for their future. If they do, it will be much brighter!

The pooling of wax in the postica-dextera quadrant
suggests a somewhat negative experience in the past.
The pooling of wax in both antica quadrants hints at a
tumultuous future, with both good and bad events;
however, the larger pooling and flow of wax into the
antica-sinistra quadrant indicates the situation will be
resolved in a very favorable way. This individual may
face some challenges, but the outcome will be great.

Again, these sample readings illustrate a general reading.

To see how a person may read a "yes or no" answer to a specific question they have asked, take another look at the last (fourth) illustration and imagine the question was, "Will I meet someone special and fall in love again?"

Looking at that last illustration, it may be that the pooling of wax in the postica-dextera quadrant reflects a bad relationship this person had in the past, one they are struggling to heal from or put behind them.

Perhaps they were hurt badly by someone or still have feelings for someone in their past. Perhaps they have to learn to trust themselves or other people again. That or something similar may be preventing them from moving forward in a new relationship.

The pooling of wax in both antica quadrants could mean that their future is going to be filled with both good and bad experiences and emotions as they seek to put this past person or relationship truly behind them and come to terms with whatever happened.

It may also be a sign that their dating life is going to have its share of ups and downs!

However, the pooling and flow of wax into the antica-sinistra (or future / yes) quadrant, is a sign that all of this will ultimately work out in the way this person wants it to—they will meet someone special and fall in love again.

So the answer is yes, but as with most things in life, there's a little more to it.

Divination: Container Candles

The walk-through I presented in this chapter can apply to almost any candle type, whether it's a paraffin wax pillar, a beeswax taper, or a multi-wax molded candle in the shape of an owl.

The basic architecture of a candle—capital, column, base—still applies, since all candles have a top, middle, and bottom!

Container candles are obviously a bit different, though. Nonetheless, you can still read the wax that congeals on the surface of the candle's capital around the wick.

Quite often, if you look closely, you will see faint lines or shapes on the cooled surface of the candle's capital: make a note of their appearance and in what quadrants they appear. You can also note the presence of any broken bits of wick on the capital and mark their location on your divination grid (wick bits are good omens).

You can also read any wax walls, deposits, accumulations, or formations that appear on the inside of the container itself.

If you see tunneling in a container candle, particularly tunneling that leans into the dextera quadrants, this can be a sign of imbalance in your life, or a sign that you are doing something self-destructive, something you have not thought through all the way.

Yet tunneling that leans or slopes to the left may be a sign that you need to be more headstrong in some area of your life, for you own good! This is why taking an intuitive and holistic view of candle reading is so important.

At the same time, tunneling can also simply mean that the wax or wick is of low quality, or that you are not burning the candle properly (this is why it's so important to follow the manufacturer's recommendations, especially if you've paid a lot for a designer candle—you want to get the most out of it).

While a container candle may not allow for the variety of wax signs that you can read in a non-container candle, it can nonetheless be a rewarding experience. This is especially so if you are treating yourself to a container candle made of an exotic wax type or blend, as these can be very interesting and pleasant to observe as they melt.

Container candles are also fabulous choices for flame-focused readings.

One reason container candles are especially valuable for flame readings is because many now boast particularly large or specialized wood wicks. These produce fantastic crackles and sizzles, with beautiful red embers and a lively, dancing flame that is mesmerizing to watch.

If you're in the mood to commune with Vesta's sacred flame, this is a wonderful way to do it. Fire always behaves differently on wood. And if you're fortunate, you may even see the flame's reflection flickering in the melted wax pool that collects at the top of the container, on the capital—if so, observe in which quadrant this happens so you can interpret this sign in context.

Higher quality or luxury container candles can also deliver fragrance that is divine.

In antiquity, the Vestals would offer fragrant incense into the sacred flame to honor the goddess with its beautiful aroma. Burning a wood wick candle that releases a strong, pleasing fragrance is therefore a lovely way to experience Vesta's flame and pay tribute to her tradition at the same time.

Similarly, the vapor released from extinguishing a fragranced container candle can be very pleasing: be sure to watch its direction carefully as it floats away, and observe the swirls for shapes.

So as you can see, while container candles may not facilitate the same variety of wax signs, they can still be very useful and revealing for candle divination. It all depends on your preferences and how you frame your question to Vesta.

What is more useful than fire?

-    Ovid, Roman Poet, 43 BCE-18 AD

CHAPTER SEVEN

Candle Wax Drippings in Water

While fire was of the utmost importance to the Vestal Virgins as they cared for Vesta's sacred hearth, water had a vital religious role to play as well. Since Vesta's fire burned continuously, there was a great deal of ash and natural charcoal to dispose of, and that had to be done with care and respect. As mentioned earlier, the priestesses therefore ritually disposed of this sacred material in the great Tiber River, essentially offering it to the river god.

It was this visual of ash and wood fragments being deposited into the water that made me want to incorporate the practice of candle wax drippings in water into my candle reading methodology. This essentially involves holding a candle over a bowl of water and letting the melting wax drip into the water. The movement and shapes of the wax drippings are then read and interpreted.

Back in chapter one, I said this practice has elements of hydromancy, yet because the water isn't being read (it's only the suspending medium), it isn't true hydromancy. Rather, it is the wax drippings that are read, which makes this form of divination fall within the scope of carromancy.

It also means that this practice aligns with my antiquity-inspired candle reading methodology that calls upon Vesta's spirit to animate the wax. And by the way, while water and very hot or boiling wax don't mix (you'd use a fire extinguisher rather than water on an out-of-control candle fire) the wax drippings here are small and cooled, as they're being dropped from above.

Selecting Your Candle

The candle you use for this method of divination should be long and thin: a taper is best, as you can hold the candle at its base and position the lit wick over the center of the bowl (at an angle, not upside down) to let wax droplets fall into the water from above.

You can also easily rotate a taper candle in your hand, to control how evenly the wax melts around the top.

Candle wax drippings in water can be a particularly fun process if you choose colored candles, since these droplets can create a sharp contrast and stand out very well in the water.

And guess what? The ancient Romans saw meaning in colors, too! Purple, for example, was (and still is) the color of royalty—only the emperor could wear a purple toga. Purple therefore symbolizes power.

White was (and still is) the color of purity. That is why the Vestals' dresses were white, as was the marble of Vesta's temple.

Yellow and orange, the traditional colors worn by a Roman bride, symbolized new beginnings, like a wedding. Spring, the season of renewal, is of course full of yellow and orange flowers.

As for the color red—well, all you have to do is picture a Roman soldier, with that great scarlet cloak, and you know what red symbolized. The color of Mars, the god of war, red suggests aggression. But that isn't all bad. Sometimes we need to be assertive and fight for our own interests, or for the interests of the vulnerable.

Red is also the color of boldness, luxury, and creativity. Pompeiian red is a deep red seen in fine ancient Roman frescos. Ochre, a rich brownish-yellow, is also a favorite.

Black was (and still is) the color of mourning. Those mourning the loss of a loved wore black, just as we do. While a black candle may on its surface appear a somber or even depressing choice, it need not be. If you are going through a mourning period or mourning the loss of something in your life, black can be a highly symbolic and cathartic color to choose, one that suits the occasion.

Green, to the Romans, symbolized the abundance of the earth (think green olive trees) as well as health. It means the same to us. The ancient Roman architect Vitruvius advocated for green spaces within cities, as these symbolized health and abundance.

Finally, multicolored or rainbow wax candles are another really fun option. These melt in strikingly beautiful ways to create a kaleidoscope of drippings. So by all means, let your creative side loose by choosing colored candles to use in this ritual!

The Divination Bowl

Ideally, your divination bowl should be either white, in honor of Vesta's temple, or clear glass: I actually prefer glass, as it allows me to see the wax droplets, straight on and at eye-level, as they move and come to rest against the sides of the bowl. Glass also lets you see the unique 3-D shapes of the wax droplets more clearly as they float. I would also recommend you choose a bowl with high vertical sides, rather than low sloped ones.

Other Divination Tools

Other than a suitable taper candle and divination bowl, you will require the same kinds of divination tools for a wax drippings in water reading as a standard pillar reading. These include a compass, wood matches, a candle snuffer, an offering and/or libation, a bit of salt, decorative stones or other markers to use as termini to establish the finis, as well as a pen and your divination grid and journal.

Methodology & Procedure

The methodology and principles of candle wax drippings in water is similar to that of other candle divination rituals. To begin, you will use east as the primary orientation and establish a finis with all of your supplies within it.

Yet instead of marking out a templum and envisioning a divination grid over the capital of a candle, you will envision those over the top of a bowl of water.

ANTICA
12 o'clock

S I N I S T R A (L) (R) **D E X T E R A**

POSTICA

The three stages of divination—invocatio, spectio, and coniectura—will proceed in much the same way here as they would in a standard pillar divination. To avoid this chapter being too redundant, I won't repeat that process in too much detail; however, you can refer back to chapter four if you need a refresher.

Suffice it to say, you will want to invoke Vesta in the proper ritualistic fashion. As always, you can ask a specific question or do a general reading, but you must state that you will await the signs within the boundaries of the bowl (although you will still observe for auspicia oblativa within and beyond the finis).

Perhaps one of the main differences is that you won't have to stipulate a time period, since candle wax drippings in water is a fairly fast ritual. You will simply drip wax into the center of the water until you are satisfied you have enough drippings to read.

As for the water you use, it should be clear and clean, without any debris in it. In antiquity, the Vestal priestesses used spring water to wash the altar in the temple, so it's important that the water you use in your divination bowl is pure. I encourage you to use bottled spring water or even rainwater.

After you invoke Vesta and light your taper, you should let it burn for a while so the wax can begin to melt. When enough wax has melted to produce droplets, hold the taper near the base and extend the column over the bowl, so the capital and flame are positioned over the center of the bowl of water. Your candle should be at a more or less 90 degree angle. You don't want the candle too upright, but you don't want it upside down either! Find a happy medium.

You should also hold your candle high enough that you can see the wax droplets falling into the water. As the candle burns in this position, you can rotate it to ensure the wax melts evenly, or in the way you find works best, around the top.

As the wax melts and the taper shortens, you can adjust the candle's position so the flame remains above the center of the water and the droplets fall in the center.

During this spectio stage, you should honor the silentium of the ritual. Remain quiet and focused on the question you are seeking an answer to, or the issue you are hoping to gain some insight into.

Do not bump or knock the bowl, as this will disturb the water—only the wax drippings should be affecting the water by their movements as they land in it and float across its surface.

If you do accidentally bump the bowl, that is a vitium. And you know what that means…the ritual must be abandoned and begun again on another day.

Even though the wax drippings are the focus of this ritual, you should still keep an eye on the behavior of the flame, always looking for signs as it burns.

When you are satisfied with the amount of wax drippings in the water, you can end this stage by thanking Vesta for her presence and extinguishing your candle. Set it safely aside.

You are now in the coniectura stage of the divination ritual, when you will read and interpret the signs.

Once the wax drippings have stopped moving and the water is still, look closely at the floating drops and wax formations.

First, record the position of the wax drippings on your divination grid. You can draw what you see in each quadrant: antica-sinistra, postica-sinistra, antica-dextera, and postica-dextera.

Second, examine the wax droplets. If they have arranged themselves into discernable or recognizable shapes, symbols, letters, or numbers, record that on your divination grid and in your journal.

If you wish, you can refer back to chapter five, where I provided you with a good inventory of symbols that included their possible meanings.

Interpretation

Interpreting a wax drippings in water reading is similar to interpreting a standard pillar candle divination. You will use the templum and divination grid in the same way to interpret what signs are favorable or unfavorable, or more significant or less significant.

You will use your imagination and intuition to find symbols or shapes, and you will especially use your intuition to find a positive, meaningful message in it all, one that you can put into the larger context of what his happening in your life.

To complete the ritual, you will take your time and make a hand-written (or type-written) summarium which will include your thoughts, feelings, interpretations, and any practical steps you are planning to take in light of your reading.

If by chance any wax drops have congealed into a shape that you find inspiring or comforting, take it out of the water and keep it! Put it on your lararium or somewhere special as a reminder that the sacred flame favors you.

Illustrations:
Sample Wax Drippings in Water Readings

I have to be honest—I love performing wax drippings in water. I find this method of reading quite addictive…I do one, then I have to do another…and then another.

I especially love doing them with friends, as we can all get in there and see what shapes or symbols we can recognize. We'll lay friendly bets on what quadrant the wax is going to move to depending on each person's particular question. We'll change the colors we use and the orientations, and see what signs appear.

There's a certain instant gratification aspect to it all. You let the wax fall and then only a few moments later you get to read the signs. If you aren't satisfied or you want to ask another question, it is easy enough to repeat the ritual with another candle and orientation. It's all right to do this, since the ancient Romans often re-took the auspices when the signs were unclear.

Yet this ritual can also be a personal and private one. A friend of mine who was going through a hard time in her life performed a wax drippings in water reading every evening for two weeks in a row.

To her, it was a way to ground herself, to stay tuned-in to her intuition, and to feel connected to a higher power. The comfort of the ritual, combined with the readings, helped her work through her problems.

The next few pages contain sample readings of wax drippings in water. The last one is particularly interesting.

While the subject of the reading saw a wax formation which she immediately recognized as a horse's head, I actually saw the number 7 in the shape. What do you see?

Regardless of what you see in the shape, this beautifully illustrates the intuitive and subjective aspect of reading the signs.

This wax drippings in water is being performed with a white taper candle. Vesta's flame is held over the center of the bowl / templum / divination grid. Wax drippings fall from above to land in the water where they can move into the various quadrants and/or form shapes. As you can see, the candle / flame is being introduced into the templum from the left (sinistra) direction, for good luck.

A wax drippings in water reading is done in largely the same way as a regular candle wax readings. Here, some drops have gathered in the postica-dextera quadrant to suggest past issues or struggles; however, the larger congealment of wax in the antica-sinistra quadrant suggests a favorable event, or significant circumstance, in this individual's future. Yellow wax was chosen to symbolize a fresh new beginning, like spring - and this reading suggested a new beginning was on its way!

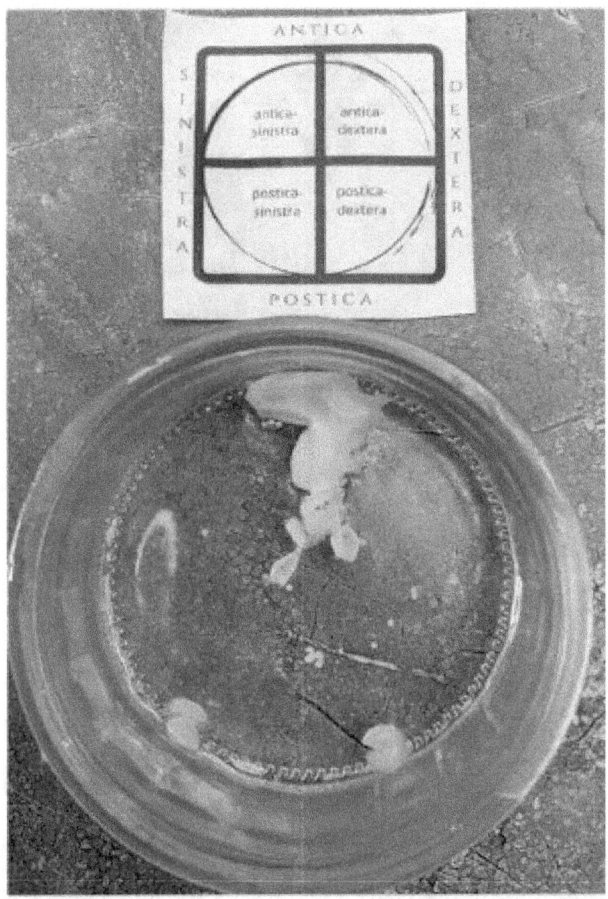

This wax drippings in water candle reading showed an interesting shape at 12 o'clock, riding the line between the antica-sinistra and antica-dextera quadrants. Is this a good or bad sign for the future? This individual saw the shape of a horse's head, a symbol of unpredictable Neptune. However, the fact that the horse is facing sinistra, or left, is a good sign! It suggests this powerful force will work for this person's benefit.

FINAL THOUGHTS

Vesta's *flamma:* Moving Forward

In the preface of this book, I asked you to light a candle and think about the question you wanted answered, or the reassurance you sought. In chapter two, we dug a little deeper.

You've come a long way since that time. Now you can light a candle, perform a proper candle divination ritual, and call upon the ancient power of Vesta's flamma to guide you in your life.

So where do you go from here? How do you incorporate what you've learned about yourself in a practical way? Because divining your life with Vesta's flame isn't about finding supernatural certainties—you aren't going to invest your money based on a candle reading. Instead, you're going to invest in *yourself*—in listening to yourself.

When you have a question or fear in life, when you're facing an uncertain path, you're going to give yourself permission, and time, to sit quietly with the sacred flame and examine the issue from all angles, so that you can make decisions that are right for you.

Personally, I think a lot of the mistakes we make in life come from not doing this. We make an impulsive decision or we just do what someone else wants us to do. Or even worse, we let fear make our decisions for us.

The ritual of a candle divination can help prevent that by forcing us to slow down and reflect upon things. The flame can spark our intuition and make us feel connected to a power that we instinctively know is greater than us. That's why Vesta's flame, and the rituals that attend it, are so important to and so central in the lives of many people who consider themselves spiritual but not religious.

While candle divination often involves seeking an answer to a question or insight into an issue, I hope you will also come to use Vesta's flame at other times too. Light it for comfort or peace.

You'll remember that the duty of Vesta's priestesses, the Vestal Virgins, was to tend the sacred flame to help maintain the pax deorum—the peaceful accord with the gods.

Don't you need peace too? When it comes to this loud, hectic, happy, confusing, disappointing, stressful, ridiculous, and amazing life....I think we all need to make our peace with it.

To me, the sacred flame is a metaphor for the eternal and enduring power of the soul. Vesta is a beautiful face in the flame, one that makes the immensity of the universe just a little more personal. I hope you'll come to think of her in the same way.

I thank you, most sincerely, for reading. And I wish you the very, very best in your life.

MORE ILLUSTRATIONS

Vesta is but living flame.

-   Ovid, Roman Poet, 43 BCE-18 AD

An auspicious sign!

This is a photo I snapped with my phone of the beeswax tealight mentioned in the preface. You can see where the column has fractured and a V-shaped wax river has flowed out. This is an ostentum, an expected yet novel and emotional sign. If you turn the photo 180° you will also see a shape that resembles a historically important bend of the Tiber River.

DIVINATION GRID:
THE TEMPLUM

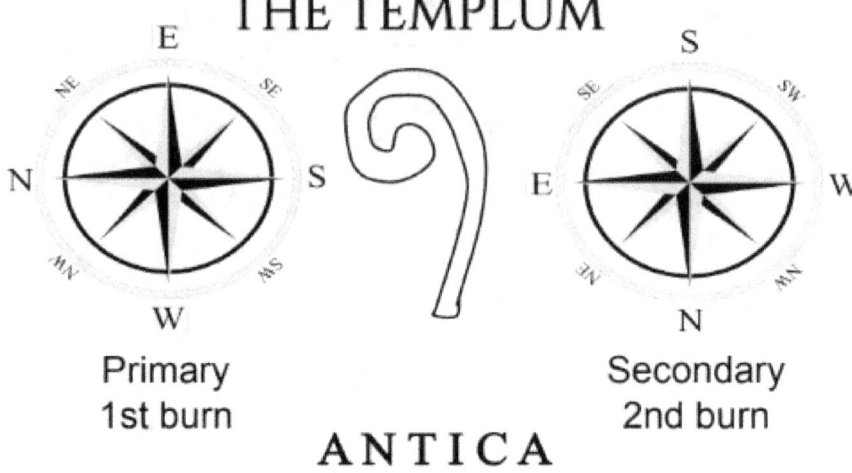

Primary
1st burn

Secondary
2nd burn

ANTICA

(antica is at 12 o'clock of candle top: wick is at center of grid)

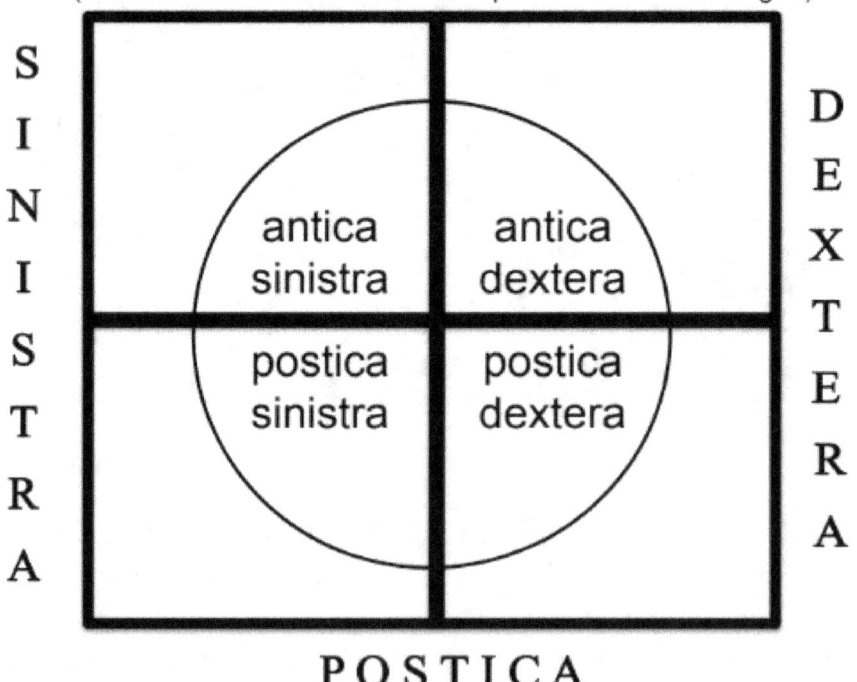

S I N I S T R A

antica
sinistra

antica
dextera

postica
sinistra

postica
dextera

D E X T E R A

POSTICA

© Debra May Macleod

Ancient Roman coin: Vesta making offering into sacred fire

Bronze statuette of Vesta, 1 – 2 century CE

Illustration of Temple of Vesta in Roman Forum

Illustration from *Justi Lipsi de Vesta et Vestalibus Syntagma* of a tool that may have captured the sun's pure rays to ignite the sacred fire

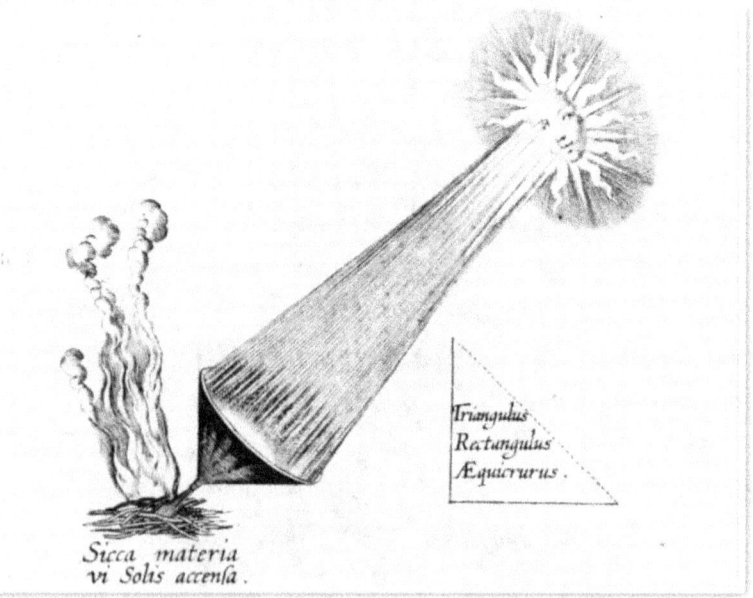

I'll leave you with a beautiful sign—a gorgeous arrangement of waxicles and spikes in the sinistra quadrants (this was a beeswax taper positioned securely in an empty wine bottle). I hope your signs are always this favorable!

For more on candle reading with Vesta's flame—there is always more to learn, and I am always expanding my foundational method and application with new aspects— please visit AllThingsVesta.com.

You'll also find Vesta-related videos, history, novels, a gallery, and simple rituals to help you welcome the ancient flame into your life, if you haven't already. Thank you and take care.